THE FOUNTAINWELL D

General Editors

T. A. DUNN

ANDREW GURR

JOHN HORDEN

A. NORMAN JEFFARES

R. L. C. LORIMER

Assistant General Editor

BRIAN W. M. SCOBIE

12

WILLIAM SHAKESPEARE

TWELFTH NIGHT OR WHAT YOU WILL

Edited by
S. MUSGROVE

OLIVER & BOYD

EDINBURGH

1969

OLIVER AND BOYD LTD
Tweeddale Court
Edinburgh 1

First published 1969

Hardback 05 001532 x
Paperback 05 001531 1

Printed in Great Britain by
Hazell Watson & Viney Ltd.
Aylesbury, Bucks

ACKNOWLEDGMENTS

Throughout the preparation of this edition I have been greatly assisted by the patience and skill, exercised over a distance of some 12,000 miles, of Mr John Horden, of Leeds University, and Mr B. W. M. Scobie, of Oliver and Boyd, in their respective roles of Textual General Editor and Assistant General Editor. Thanks are due to both.

S. M.

Auckland,
New Zealand,
1968

CONTENTS

CRITICAL INTRODUCTION

Twelfth Night was probably written in 1601. It is not in the list of Shakespeare's plays given by Meres in his *Palladis Tamia* (1598). On 2 Feb. 1602, John Manningham of the Middle Temple recorded in his diary (if the entry is authentic, which is not quite certain) that he saw it played "at our feast". He noted its likeness to Plautus' *Menaechmi*, and to an Italian play called by him *Inganni*. He clearly enjoyed it, though he got the impression that Olivia was a widow. The play was obviously new to him; we do not know whether there was an earlier performance. This date agrees with probable references to Wright's "new map" of the world, dated *c.*1600 (III. II. 67), and to Shirley's voyage to Persia (II. v. 152), and with the appearance of "Farewell dear heart" in Robert Jones's *First Booke of Ayres* (1600).[1] In general, the play leaves the impression of being the most mature of the romantic comedies.

In *The First Night of Twelfth Night* Hotson makes an elaborate case for a first performance, arena-style, at Whitehall on Twelfth Night (6 Jan.), 1601, when the Queen entertained Virginio Orsino, Duke of Bracciano, the small boy of *The White Devil*, with a "mingled comedy, with pieces of music and dances". The documents discovered by Hotson unhappily do not describe the play, and his dating implies that it was written, rehearsed, and produced in twelve days. In this view Olivia is an idealised young Elizabeth, Orsino a version of Bracciano, and Malvolio a caricature of Sir William Knollys, Controller of the Royal Household. There are many court jokes and references. Though Hotson illuminates many details, it is doubtful whether a touchy ducal visitor would have been pleased with a portrait of himself

[1] Edward Wright's map is found in some copies of Hakluyt, *Principal Navigations* (1598–1600). Sir Anthony Shirley visited the Shah of Persia in 1599, bringing back rich gifts. An account of his voyage was printed by Oct. 1600, but suppressed till Sep. 1601. The song may well be earlier. G. B. Harrison puts the case for Shakespeare's use of Samuel Harsnett's *Discovery of the Fraudulent Practises of John Darrell* (a Puritan exorcist), published 1599, and a reply of 1600. See G. B. Harrison, *Shakespeare at Work*, pp. 291 ff. The question of revision is discussed in the Note on the Text.

as a sentimental lover. It is more likely that Shakespeare, working on the play in 1601, took advantage of Orsino's visit to cast a few sly glances, at Knollys among others.

The story of muddled twins comes originally from Plautus' *Menaechmi*. Shakespeare had improved on this in *Comedy of Errors*, given as a Christmas play at Gray's Inn in 1594, and he must have recalled the Pinch scene (IV. iv), which reads like an early sketch for Sir Topas' examination of Malvolio. When one twin is a girl, who disguises herself as a page to serve the man she loves (cp. *Two Gentlemen of Verona*), the basic formula is complete. This formula appears in some dozen sixteenth-century versions, narrative and dramatic, and we cannot be sure which Shakespeare used. Probably he knew *Gl'Ingannati* (1537), a bustling Sienese comedy written by a group called the *Intronati* ("Thunderstruck")[2], and also Barnaby Riche's narrative "Of Apolonius and Silla" in *Riche His Farewell to Militarie Profession* (1581), which has a Duke, a shipwreck, and an eastern Mediterranean setting. In Emanuel Forde's novel *Parismus* (1598) the disguised page is called Violetta, and there is an Olivia. Other versions include Secchi's *Gl'Inganni* (1562), another *Gl'Inganni* (1592) by Gonzaga, Estienne's *Les Abusés* (1543), a Latin *Lælia* (c.1545), and narrative versions in Bandello's *Novelle* (1554) and Belleforest's *Histoires Tragiques*, vol. IV (1579). Secchi's *L'Interesse* (published 1581) may have provided Viola's duel.[3] These versions cover only the main plot, the rest, apart from a few hints, being Shakespeare's own. They are essentially unpoetical; more realistic than *Twelfth Night*, but infinitely less real.

The play requires no use of the upper level, or of the discovery

---

[2] See G. Bullough, *Narrative and Dramatic Sources of Shakespeare*, II. 269–372, for fuller details. Manningham's "*Inganni*" was probably an error for "*Gl' Ingannati*". The names in *Gl'Ingannati* are: Lelia (Fabio) = Viola (Cesario); Flamminio = Orsino; Isabella = Olivia; Fabrizio = Sebastian. Fabio may have given Fabian (though "fabian" is Elizabethan English for "swashbuckler"). Malevolti in the *preludium* may have given Malvolio, though this name, as Bullough says, is merely the converse of the good-hearted Benvolio of *Romeo and Juliet*. The joke on "accost" may have come from here, and also the idea of Twelfth Night: see Bullough, *op. cit.* II. 290, 298, 307–8. Cesario seems to come from Gonzaga's Cesare.

[3] See H. A. Kaufman, "Nicolò Secchi as a Source of *Twelfth Night*", in *Shakespeare Quarterly*, V (1954), pp. 271–80. Secchi's treatment of the comic heroine is not unlike Shakespeare's.

space (the so-called "inner" stage).[4] It may have been written either for the public theatre or a hall, and it is only an improbable guess that De Witt's drawing of the Swan theatre shows Malvolio, staff and all, confronting Olivia and Maria. Feste, like Touchstone and Lear's fool, was doubtless created for Robert Armin, the "clown" who took Kemp's place in the company about 1599, and for his sensitive comic style. There is no evidence of the original casting. We hear of court performances in 1618 and 1623, when the play was called *Malvolio*, a sure sign of what people liked. After the Restoration, it passed to the Duke's company, and was seen by Pepys, who found it "silly". Like most of the comedies, it then fell out of fashion. In 1741, Macklin played it at Drury Lane, and thereafter it held its place, though sometimes competing with musical versions. Charles Lamb remembered with delight one of the famous Violas, Dora Jordan, who played as late as 1808. Productions in the nineteenth century were legion: the Stratford and Saxe-Meiningen companies both gave it in 1881, Irving in 1884, the Elizabethan Stage Society in 1895, Tree in 1901, Granville-Barker, amid controversy, in 1912, and the Old Vic in its first season of 1914. In 1950, re-opening after ten years of war-time darkness, the Old Vic chose it as its first production.

Like Jane Austen's novels, Shakespeare's romantic comedies treat of the "moral art of securing happiness" in love.[5] *Twelfth Night* is the richest and subtlest of them, as it is latest in time. Traditional stage devices like indistinguishable twins, a boy heroine, and improbable coincidences do not render the play "silly" or irrelevant. They make poetical speech easier. They typify the unpredictable currents of "fortune" in the world, and they are figuratively apt to the psychology of the play, since human love is a matter of disguises and confused identities. *Twelfth Night* is funny and serious, and the broader comedy (too germane to be called an underplot) anchors it to coarse fact.

The Saturnalian Twelfth Night was a time of licensed misrule, disorder, and inversion, ritualised into Christmas games. The play contains little that is directly referable to this festival, but in spirit it is akin: women woo men, servants marry masters, wisdom and folly

[4] R. Watkins places the box-tree scene in the discovery space, but this is very doubtful. See R. Watkins, *On Producing Shakespeare*, p. 138. G. P. V. Akrigg, "*Twelfth Night* at the Middle Temple", in *Shakespeare Quarterly*, IX (1958) pp. 422–4, argues that the Temple production was the first.

[5] H. B. Charlton, *Shakespearian Comedy*, p. 290.

shift like the colours of an opal. The alternative title, *What You Will* (if it is not a mere throw-away) points to the heart of the matter: to the wilfulness of human action and desire.[6] What is looked for in men and women is enunciated by Olivia: "to be generous, guiltless, and of free disposition". The opposite quality, for which Malvolio is rejected more harshly than Falstaff, is to be "sick of self-love", to "taste with a distempered appetite".

Malvolio is the clearest case. In Act V he is allowed to speak in his own cause without self-pity or absurdity: but he goes off unreconciled because he can neither love nor forgive. His fantasies of marriage with Olivia are strongly sensual; what cannot be pardoned in them is that they are self-bounded, reducing Olivia to a property. Malvolio, as well as being pompous and ridiculous, is also honest and responsible: but it is because he has the cold pride of the self-righteous that he is the proper subject for comic scorn and rebuke. Like Jaques, he is near to a Jonsonian character, but he is in no sense "tragic".

Malvolio is not attacked as a specimen Puritan—Maria makes this clear when she calls him "a *kind* of Puritan": but some of his qualities are like those of the Puritan stereotype. His aspiration for Olivia's hand is not as farcically absurd as it often appears on stage. The steward of a great countess was often a gentleman by birth, and in her absence reigned supreme over her whole household. Malvolio is to be thought of as belonging to the same social class as Maria, Andrew, Fabian, and Toby: minor gentry, attached to the great house, but not menial dependents of it. The comic business of the "lighter people" is not knockabout; it takes place one social rung below the main events and, as Toby sees, runs dangerously close to serious trouble.

Toby is not to be imagined as a sodden old man, nor as a Falstaff *manqué*. His love of a practical joke is a habit of his class. He is apparently capable of being salvaged, since Maria, witty and intelligent—and presumably guiltless and free—marries him at the end. The few places where he speaks unliquored show his intelligence and breeding. He lives at ease by virtue of being "consanguineous"; his drunkenness is both his liberty and his bondage. To prey on a thing so defenceless as Andrew argues a thick hide, but is good enough for a May morning. Andrew is the most stupid character in all Shakespeare—so null that there is not even a serving wench provided for his comfort at the end.

---

[6] See S. Nagarajan, " 'What You Will': A Suggestion", in *Shakespeare Quarterly*, X (1959), pp. 61–7.

His one virtue is that, unlike the cleverer people, he is pretty sure that he is a fool, though stoutly hoping to be proved wrong. There is no reason to see him as a *nouveau riche*.

On the serious side, the one relationship that is uncomplicated and unmasked is that between Sebastian and Antonio: the young man's hero-worship of the elder, and the elder's "dedication" to the vulnerable perfection of youth. When Sebastian seems to break this bond, Antonio's anger is genuine and deep, since of "any taint of vice whose strong corruption Inhabits our frail blood", the ugliest is "ingratitude". It has been well observed that this friendship recalls the mood of the Sonnets;[7] its threatened breach also anticipates *Lear*.

The four lovers (despite the stage tradition which preserves a rather buxom Olivia) are all to be thought of as very young. Any faults in them are as venial as Romeo's adolescent hysteria or his calf-love for Rosaline. Orsino and Olivia are both "noble" people. Unlike Malvolio, they are capable of self-correction, of learning who and what they are under the discipline and laughter of love. Their wilful luxuriating in sentiment no doubt comes from reading too much Petrarch, or perhaps Sidney; Viola, masked in the reality of stage disguise, releases them from bondage. Olivia, spoilt, charming, and self-willed, has the simpler lesson to learn: that she is in fact a "healthy and nubile woman",[8] longing for the "one self king" her "sweet perfections" lack. The growth of her love for Cesario, modest and passionate, is natural and, in the ironic context, moving. If, like Johnson, we are concerned that her speedy nuptials lack "credibility", we may remember that she rushes Sebastian into matrimony when frightened out of her wits by Toby's formidable sword. The male spirit of Orsino is more troubled and complex. He is drawn with the tongue in the cheek. His language is ironically inflated, too consciously literary. But, though it is true that he savours his own emotions, that he is in love with love, he is no mawkish amateur of music. The imagery of his speeches is sometimes disturbing: his appetites are as hungry as the sea, he speaks of "cloyment" and "revolt", he calls Olivia "marble-breasted", as the fiend in *Lear* is "marble-hearted", and he can imagine (though out of a novel) killing what he loves. Yet this tide of emotion

---

[7] See M. M. Mahood, "Love's Confined Doom", in *Shakespeare Survey*, xv (1962), pp. 55–6.

[8] G. K. Hunter, "The Later Comedies", in *Shakespeare, The Writer and his Work*, ed. B. Dobrée, p. 230.

is decorum in a great duke, and in the man and the context understandable as the fruits of "injured vanity".[9] If we think that he is not good enough for Viola, we should remember that it is the woman's role to "sway level" in her husband's heart, and by her sweetness and common sense to prevent his strength (and his folly) from breaking out into "uncivil" violence.

Viola rises, like Venus, from the sea, and though we never again see her as a woman, we know perfectly what she is. She is kin to Rosalind, but kinder and more alone. Whereas Olivia, in her early mood, is niggard of her love, Viola gives of her wealth[10] with total frankness and truth: but also with intelligence, wit, and that familiar grasp of things as they are which is the mark of the heroine of Shakespearian comedy. Her modesty, friendliness, and courage are all present in the unspoilt form of youth; and she can endure being laughed at because she never pretends. But she is also an accomplished actress, playing a courtly and romantic role with a fine flourish. In *Twelfth Night* as in *Hamlet*, written much about the same time, Shakespeare is concerned with the shifting faces of appearance and reality, and in both plays with the puzzling nature of theatrical illusion. Viola avers that she is no "comedian"—yet, "I am not that I play"; she is disguised, but she does not "usurp herself". In the upshot, human truth is only made clear by the devices of the theatrical mask.[11]

In Elizabethan thinking, love is a species of melancholy, and the symptoms shown by Olivia, Orsino, and the incurable Malvolio are all diagnosed by Burton. Both Rosalind and Romeo tell us that "love is merely a madness", deserving a "dark house and a whip as madmen do", and lovers "bound more than a madman is, ... whipped and tormented";[12] and in *Hamlet* love-madness is a constituent of tragedy. *Twelfth Night* just brushes on this painful area, set as it is "on the borders of wonder and madness".[13] Therefore, over the whole play, the presiding spirit is that of the wise fool, Feste. He is so important

---

[9] L. G. Salingar, "The Design of Twelfth Night", in *Shakespeare Quarterly*, IX (1958), p. 125. This article (pp. 117–39) is a valuable and detailed study.

[10] See J. R. Brown, *Shakespeare and his Comedies*, pp. 160–82.

[11] For a wholly different reading of the play, by which the lovers marry prudentially under the demands of the Elizabethan social code, see J. W. Draper, *The Twelfth Night of Shakespeare's Audience*.

[12] *As You Like It*, III. II. 396 ff.; *Romeo and Juliet*, I. II. 54.

[13] F. Kermode, "The Mature Comedies", in *Stratford-upon-Avon Studies*, VI (1961), p. 227.

to the design that Shakespeare gives Viola a set speech analysing the wisdom of the fool's art in terms that come near to defining dramatic decorum itself.[14] Feste is attached firmly to neither household—indeed, he lives "by the church"—but is familiar in both, as folly is universal. He is the professional "corrupter of words" to the nobility, ready to prove by logic that wisdom and folly are interchangeable terms.[15] Though he has his mistress, he is not, like Touchstone, a candidate for the folly of matrimony, and indeed eschews all participation in the action except for the theatrical role of Sir Topas. Unlike Lear's fool, he gives no hostages to fortune in the way of affection—even to Viola—or loyalty; and his final song, whether written by Armin or by Shakespeare, sounds very much like whistling in the dark. The world began a long time ago. Its constants are the wind and the rain—and also human behaviour, whatever you like to call it. For a moment, it can be caught by the patterned follies and confusions, the music and the disharmony, of a festive play—"our play". But now that is "done". This is the end of a series, the last of the comedies of the "golden time".

[14] III. I. 58 ff.; see M. C. Bradbrook, *Shakespeare and Elizabethan Poetry*, p. 232. G. B. Harrison, *Shakespeare at Work*, p. 295, argues that the lines are based on some of Armin's own, published in 1600.

[15] C. J. Sisson points out that in Elizabethan English the legal term meaning the opposite of "idiot" is "wise man": "Tudor Intelligence Tests: Malvolio and Real Life", in *Essays on Shakespeare and Elizabethan Drama*, ed. R. Hosley, p. 188.

A NOTE ON THE TEXT

Twelfth Night was first published in the Folio of 1623, being entered in the Stationers' Register on 8 Nov. 1623 to Blount and Jaggard among the plays "not formerly entred to other men". F is the only text of primary significance. The present edition is based on the B. M. copy C. 21 e. 16, collated with the copy in the Auckland Public Library (whose copies of F2, F3, and F4 I have also consulted) and with the facsimiles of F edited by Lee, Kökeritz, and Dover Wilson. In all nearly 250 copies of F are known to exist.

The play occupies pp. 255–75 (first pagination), Y2r–Z6r. Hinman notes the occurrence of a break in the printing of F after quire X (*All's Well*), suggesting that the copy for *Twelfth Night*, as for *A Winter's Tale*, was not "readily available". The printer went on to quires a and b (*King John*), and then back to *Twelfth Night*. This stage in the printing took place in October/November 1622. The play was set up by compositor B—the man responsible for the bulk of F—from case y. Hinman finds no evidence for proof-correction in quire Y, and only three trifling non-textual variants in quire Z.[1] The satyr ornament at the end, evidentially important, was damaged during the printing of *Twelfth Night*; its differing states provide evidence for the order of printing, not only of parts of F, but for some other books in Jaggard's shop.

The F text of *Twelfth Night*, by comparison with many other plays in the volume, is clean and well-ordered, with no confusion as to names, though the stage directions are very bare. It is fully divided into acts and scenes. The S.D. for II. II ("*Enter . . . at seuerall doores*") indicates copy of playhouse provenance. This may have been a prompt-book, but the clean text more probably suggests a transcript. The formulæ at the end of Acts I, II, and IV ("*Finis Actus Quartus*", etc.) are almost unique in F, being paralleled only by "*Finis Actus Primus*"

---

[1] C. Hinman, *The Printing and Proof-Reading of the First Folio of Shakespeare*, II. 480–6, 521. There are, however, signs of closing and straightening of type on p. 256 in the facsimiles (not in the B. M. or Auckland copies), and the Variorum edition records some untypical minutiæ on pp. 255 and 256.

in *Love's Labour's Lost*, and *Finis* at the end of Act I of *Two Gentlemen of Verona*. Such formulæ can, of course, be found in texts before 1600, but since the regular division into five acts, certainly for public theatre plays, was not established till some years after 1600, their unusual occurrence in F may be some evidence of a late date, and therefore of a transcript. The text employs neither the dash nor the exclamation point, which again may point to the scrupulosity of a professional scribe.[2]

The error at I. v. 147, "*Enter Violenta*" (for "*Viola*") need be no more than a muddle for "*Viola enter*", though there is a silent and anomalous Violenta in *All's Well*, in addition to the Violetta of *Parismus*. Curio, though named in the entry, has no lines in Act V; but there is no need to see signs of revision in this, since he enters as a member of the court.

Certain anomalies in the plot have long been noted. At II. III. 153 the plan is for Feste to join in the gulling of Malvolio, whereas in II. v it is Fabian who, without explanation, "makes a third". Then, in II. IV, where there are signs of awkwardness in the dialogue, Feste is brought in to sing "Come away death", when, it is argued, Viola is the natural person to sing it (cp. I. II. 59–60). Therefore, in his edition of 1930 (pp. 91 ff.), Dover Wilson, following Noble, held that originally Viola sang the songs, and that by 1606 (perhaps when the boy's voice had broken) Armin's fame as a singer and as Lear's fool was such that the songs were transferred to him, and the final song—probably of his own composition—added. This necessitated a corresponding "lightening" of his part, and a revision of the play in which Fabian was substituted for him in some scenes.

Though many have followed this view, the case, already attacked by S. L. Bethell,[3] does not stand up well. Fabian's lines in II. v and elsewhere are all completely in character for him and out of character for Feste;[4] a very detailed rewriting of this part must have taken place

---

[2] Not more than four other F plays show this feature: *Measure for Measure*, *The Comedy of Errors*, *King John*, and *Henry V*: but they are not textually alike. I have been compelled to introduce the dash for clarity in a very few places, but have avoided the exclamation point throughout. The query, of course, often indicates an exclamation.

[3] *Shakespeare and the Popular Dramatic Tradition*, pp. 137–44. In *Shakespeare's Happy Comedies*, p. 165, Dover Wilson's brief account of the revision seems to suggest a modification of his view towards only "slight" changes.

[4] An opposite view is held by Roy Walker, "The Whirligig of Time", in *Shakespeare Survey*, XII (1959), pp. 128, 130.

without leaving any traces, which is inherently improbable. The design of the play is such that Viola could never have sung any of the songs except perhaps that in II. IV. The way in which Feste wanders between the two great houses is, as Dover Wilson himself notes, solidly built into the play by passages in I. V, II. I, and V. I, and is figuratively necessary as a sign of the universality of folly. A close examination of II. III reveals other oddities in it, in addition to the plan for Feste to "make a third". Thus at ll. 113–117, it is proposed that Andrew should issue a challenge not to Viola but to Malvolio— the embryo of a delicious comic idea, fated to remain unborn. When Maria enters, she warns the others that Olivia will summon "her Steward *Malvolio*" (l. 67), and a little later (ll. 124 ff.), when Toby invites her to "tell us something of him", she describes his character in a set piece. But neither Toby nor the audience needs to be told that Malvolio is a steward, since he has already appeared in I. V, nor is his character unknown, since it has already been exhibited. The passage in II. III in fact looks like an example of the standard technique (cp. *Much Ado*, I. I) by which the audience is familiarised with a character before his first appearance. It may then be that this scene, or part of it, was written very early in the play's composition, before Shakespeare had settled all the details of the plot. Further thought showed the obvious need for a "straight man" for the plotting, and so Fabian was invented and Feste left out of II. V—an omission which is in fact demanded by his character.

There is thus no need to imagine any major revision.[5] There may have been some slight alteration in II. IV. Maybe Viola did originally sing here; or there may originally have been no song at all, but only music as in the opening scene. In that case, the additions are ll. 2–13 and 45–77, and the awkward join is visible at ll. 1–2, where the repeated "Now . . ." has long bothered editors. If the final song is by Armin—though most now find it Shakespearian—it could have been added at any time. Presumably, as in other plays, the 1606 blasphemy law has operated, accounting for the frequent appearance of "Jove" for "God", especially in Malvolio's speeches, though this may be in character.

Dover Wilson further suggests that II. I, in which the prose seems

[5] Unless we believe with Dover Wilson, *Twelfth Night*, pp. 97 ff., that some passages (*e.g.*, III. I. 20 ff.) must have been written about 1606 because of their relevance to the "equivocation" controversy.

over-written for its function, resembles some doubtful scenes in *Measure for Measure*, and was written by a "dramatic journeyman". But Sebastian's speech in general seems slightly over-fashionable, and this may have been intended.[6]

The text of F has here been followed closely, changes being made only for what seem to me positive errors, or (very occasionally in the punctuation) for the imperative needs of clarity. The modern form has been silently adopted for i/j, u/v, w/vv, long and short s, and for standard abbreviations like "y^u". Also, "&" appears as "and", "&c." as "etc." In stage-directions and speech-headings, names are capitalised and spelt out in full. Otherwise the F forms in stage directions are followed throughout, except that "Clowne" is standardised as "CLOWN", "Anthonio" as "ANTONIO" (this being the form used at his first appearance), and the knights are always allowed their "SIR". These changes are made silently, as is the addition of a Dramatis Personae; other editorial alterations in stage directions are indicated by pointed brackets ⟨⟩. Square brackets [ ] are used to enclose F stage directions which occur within a speech. All other changes from F are shown in the textual notes, except for such minutiæ as turned and wrong-fount letters, the omission of a capital in, or a stop after, "*Exit*" and the like, the use of a comma after a speech-heading, or of the italic forms of the query or the parenthesis. These are not recorded.

[6] But in this scene the spelling "Antonio" is used, whereas elsewhere (except once in III. IV) the spelling is "Anthonio".

DRAMATIS PERSONAE

(In order of appearance)

DUKE, *Orsino, Duke of Illyria*

CURIO, *a lord*

VALENTINE, *a Gentleman*

VIOLA

CAPTAIN

SIR TOBY BELCH

MARIA, *a Gentlewoman*

SIR ANDREW AGUECHEEK

CLOWN

OLIVIA, *a Countess*

MALVOLIO, *her Steward*

ANTONIO, *a Sea-captain*

SEBASTIAN, *twin brother to Viola*

FABIAN, *a Gentleman*

SERVANT

OFFICERS

PRIEST

LORDS, SAILORS, ATTENDANTS, MUSICIANS

THE SCENE: Illyria—the sea-coast, and habitations nearby

ACT I

Enter ORSINO, DUKE *of Illyria*, CURIO, *and other Lords.*
〈*Music is heard, then ceases.*〉

DUKE.   If Musicke be the food of Love, play on,
Give me excesse of it: that surfetting,
The appetite may sicken, and so dye.
That straine agen, it had a dying fall:
O, it came ore my eare, like the sweet sound
That breathes upon a banke of Violets;
Stealing, and giving Odour.

〈*Music again.*〉

                    Enough, no more,
'Tis not so sweet now, as it was before.
O spirit of Love, how quicke and fresh art thou,
That notwithstanding thy capacitie   10
Receiveth as the Sea, nought enters there,
Of what validity, and pitch so ere,
But falles into abatement, and low price
Even in a minute; so full of shapes is fancie,
That it alone, is high fantasticall.   15
CURIO.   Will you go hunt my Lord?
DUKE.   What *Curio*?
CURIO.   The Hart.
DUKE.   Why so I do, the Noblest that I have:
O when mine eyes did see *Olivia* first,   20
Me thought she purg'd the ayre of pestilence;
That instant was I turn'd into a Hart,
And my desires like fell and cruell hounds,
Ere since pursue me.

Enter VALENTINE.
                    How now what newes from her?

VALENTINE.   So please my Lord, I might not be admitted,   25
   But from her handmaid do returne this answer:
   The Element it selfe, till seven yeares heate,
   Shall not behold her face at ample view:
   But like a Cloystresse she will vailed walke,
   And water once a day her Chamber round   30
   With eye-offending brine: all this to season
   A brothers dead love, which she would keepe fresh
   And lasting, in her sad remembrance.
DUKE.   O she that hath a heart of that fine frame
   To pay this debt of love but to a brother,   35
   How will she love, when the rich golden shaft
   Hath kill'd the flocke of all affections else
   That live in her. When Liver, Braine, and Heart,
   These soveraigne thrones, are all supply'd and fill'd
   Her sweete perfections with one selfe king: 40
   Away before me, to sweet beds of Flowres,
   Love-thoughts lye rich, when canopy'd with bowres.

                                        Exeunt.

⟨SCENE II⟩

Enter VIOLA, *a* CAPTAINE, *and* SAYLORS.

VIOLA.   What Country (Friends) is this?
CAPTAINE.   This is Illyria Ladie.
VIOLA.   And what should I do in Illyria?
   My brother he is in Elizium,
   Perchance he is not drown'd: What thinke you saylors?   5
CAPTAINE.   It is perchance that you your selfe were saved.
VIOLA.   O my poore brother, and so perchance may he be.
CAPTAINE.   True Madam, and to comfort you with chance,
   Assure your selfe, after our ship did split,
   When you, and those poore number saved with you,   10
   Hung on our driving boate: I saw your brother
   Most provident in perill, binde himselfe,
   (Courage and hope both teaching him the practise)
   To a strong Maste, that liv'd upon the sea:
   Where like *Arion* on the Dolphines backe,   15

I saw him hold acquaintance with the waves,
So long as I could see.
VIOLA.　For saying so, there's Gold:
Mine owne escape unfoldeth to my hope,
Whereto thy speech serves for authoritie,　　　　20
The like of him. Know'st thou this Countrey?
CAPTAINE.　I Madam well, for I was bred and borne
Not three houres travaile from this very place.
VIOLA.　Who governes heere?
CAPTAINE.　A noble Duke in nature, as in name.　　25
VIOLA.　What is his name?
CAPTAINE.　*Orsino.*
VIOLA.　*Orsino*: I have heard my father name him.
He was a Batchellor then.
CAPTAINE.　And so is now, or was so very late:　　30
For but a month ago I went from hence,
And then 'twas fresh in murmure (as you know
What great ones do, the lesse will prattle of,)
That he did seeke the love of faire *Olivia.*
VIOLA.　What's shee?　　　　35
CAPTAINE.　A vertuous maid, the daughter of a Count
That dide some twelvemonth since, then leaving her
In the protection of his sonne, her brother,
Who shortly also dide: for whose deere love
(They say) she hath abjur'd the sight　　　　40
And company of men.
VIOLA.　O that I serv'd that Lady,
And might not be delivered to the world
Till I had made mine owne occasion mellow
What my estate is.　　　　45
CAPTAINE.　That were hard to compasse,
Because she will admit no kinde of suite,
No, not the Dukes.
VIOLA.　There is a faire behaviour in thee Captaine,
And though that nature, with a beauteous wall　　50
Doth oft close in pollution: yet of thee
I will beleeve thou hast a minde that suites
With this thy faire and outward charracter.
I prethee (and Ile pay thee bounteously)

Conceale me what I am, and be my ayde,   55
For such disguise as haply shall become
The forme of my intent. Ile serve this Duke,
Thou shalt present me as an Eunuch to him,
It may be worth thy paines: for I can sing,
And speake to him in many sorts of Musicke,   60
That will allow me very worth his service.
What else may hap, to time I will commit,
Onely shape thou thy silence to my wit.

CAPTAINE.   Be you his Eunuch, and your Mute Ile bee,
When my tongue blabs, then let mine eyes not see.   65

VIOLA.   I thanke thee: Lead me on.

Exeunt.

⟨SCENE III⟩

Enter SIR TOBY, *and* MARIA.

SIR TOBY.   What a plague meanes my Neece to take the death of
her brother thus? I am sure care's an enemie to life.

MARIA.   By my troth sir *Toby*, you must come in earlyer a nights:
your Cosin, my Lady, takes great exceptions to your ill houres.

SIR TOBY.   Why let her except, before excepted.   5

MARIA.   I, but you must confine your selfe within the modest
limits of order.

SIR TOBY.   Confine? Ile confine my selfe no finer then I am:
these cloathes are good enough to drinke in, and so bee these
boots too: and they be not, let them hang themselves in their   10
owne straps.

MARIA.   That quaffing and drinking will undoe you: I heard my
Lady talke of it yesterday: and of a foolish knight that you
brought in one night here, to be hir woer.

SIR TOBY.   Who, Sir *Andrew Ague-cheeke*?   15

MARIA.   I he.

SIR TOBY.   He's as tall a man as any's in Illyria.

MARIA.   What's that to th'purpose?

SIR TOBY.   Why he ha's three thousand ducates a yeare.

MARIA.   I, but hee'l have but a yeare in all these ducates: He's a   20
very foole, and a prodigall.

SIR TOBY.   Fie, that you'l say so: he playes o'th Viol-de-gam-

boys, and speaks three or four languages word for word without
booke, and hath all the good gifts of nature.

MARIA.   He hath indeed, almost naturall: for besides that he's a   25
foole, he's a great quarreller: and but that hee hath the gift of a
Coward, to allay the gust he hath in quarrelling, 'tis thought
among the prudent, he would quickely have the gift of a grave.

SIR TOBY.   By this hand they are scoundrels and substractors that
say so of him. Who are they?   30

MARIA.   They that adde moreover, hee's drunke nightly in your
company.

SIR TOBY.   With drinking healths to my Neece: Ile drinke to her
as long as there is a passage in my throat, and drinke in Illyria:
he's a Coward and a Coystrill that will not drinke to my Neece,   35
till his braines turne o'th toe, like a parish top. What wench?
Castiliano vulgo: for here coms Sir *Andrew Agueface*.

Enter SIR ANDREW.

SIR ANDREW.   Sir *Toby Belch*. How now sir *Toby Belch*?

SIR TOBY.   Sweet sir *Andrew*.

SIR ANDREW.   Blesse you faire Shrew.   40

MARIA.   And you too sir.

SIR TOBY.   Accost Sir *Andrew*, accost.

SIR ANDREW.   What's that?

SIR TOBY.   My Neeces Chamber-maid.

SIR ANDREW.   Good Mistris Accost, I desire better acquaintance.   45

MARIA.   My name is *Mary* sir.

SIR ANDREW.   Good mistris *Mary* Accost.

SIR TOBY.   You mistake knight: Accost, is front her, boord her,
woe her, assayle her.

SIR ANDREW.   By my troth I would not undertake her in this   50
company. Is that the meaning of Accost?

MARIA.   Far you well Gentlemen.

SIR TOBY.   And thou let part so Sir *Andrew*, would thou mightst
never draw sword agen.

SIR ANDREW.   And you part so mistris, I would I might never   55
draw sword agen: Faire Lady, doe you thinke you have fooles in
hand?

MARIA.   Sir, I have not you by'th hand.

SIR ANDREW.   Marry but you shall have, and heeres my hand.

MARIA. Now sir, thought is free: I pray you bring your hand   60
to'th Buttry barre, and let it drinke.

SIR ANDREW. Wherefore (sweet-heart?) What's your Metaphor?

MARIA. It's dry sir.

SIR ANDREW. Why I thinke so: I am not such an asse, but I can   65
keepe my hand dry. But what's your jest?

MARIA. A dry jest Sir.

SIR ANDREW. Are you full of them?

MARIA. I Sir, I have them at my fingers ends: marry now I let go
your hand, I am barren.

Exit MARIA.   70

SIR TOBY. O knight, thou lack'st a cup of Canarie: when did
I see thee so put downe?

SIR ANDREW. Never in your life I thinke, unlesse you see
Canarie put me downe: mee thinkes sometimes I have no more
wit then a Christian, or an ordinary man ha's: but I am a great   75
eater of beefe, and I beleeve that does harme to my wit.

SIR TOBY. No question.

SIR ANDREW. And I thought that, I'de forsweare it. Ile ride
home to morrow sir *Toby*.

SIR TOBY. *Pur-quoy* my deere knight?   80

SIR ANDREW. What is *purquoy*? Do, or not do? I would I had
bestowed that time in the tongues, that I have in fencing, dancing, and beare-bayting: O had I but followed the Arts.

SIR TOBY. Then hadst thou had an excellent head of haire.

SIR ANDREW. Why, would that have mended my haire?   85

SIR TOBY. Past question, for thou seest it will not curle by
nature.

SIR ANDREW. But it becomes me wel enough, dos't not?

SIR TOBY. Excellent, it hangs like flax on a distaffe: and I hope
to see a huswife take thee between her legs, and spin it off.   90

SIR ANDREW. Faith Ile home to morrow sir *Toby*, your niece
wil not be seene, or if she be it's four to one, she'l none of me:
the Count himselfe here hard by, wooes her.

SIR TOBY. Shee'l none o'th Count, she'l not match above hir
degree, neither in estate, yeares, nor wit: I have heard her swear't.   95
Tut there's life in't man.

I. III. 86 curle by nature.] THEOBALD; coole my nature_Λ F.

SIR ANDREW.   Ile stay a moneth longer. I am a fellow o'th strang-
 est minde i'th world: I delight in Maskes and Revels sometimes
 altogether.

SIR TOBY.   Art thou good at these kicke-chawses Knight?   100

SIR ANDREW.   As any man in Illyria, whatsoever he be, under
 the degree of my betters, and yet I will not compare with an old
 man.

SIR TOBY.   What is thy excellence in a galliard, knight?

SIR ANDREW.   Faith, I can cut a caper.   105

SIR TOBY.   And I can cut the Mutton too't.

SIR ANDREW.   And I thinke I have the backe-tricke, simply as
 strong as any man in Illyria.

SIR TOBY.   Wherefore are these things hid? Wherefore have
 these gifts a Curtaine before 'em? Are they like to take dust, like   110
 mistris *Mals* picture? Why dost thou not goe to Church in a
 Galliard, and come home in a Carranto? My verie walke should
 be a Jigge: I would not so much as make water but in a Sinke-a-
 pace: What dooest thou meane? Is it a world to hide vertues in?
 I did thinke by the excellent constitution of thy legge, it was   115
 form'd under the starre of a Galliard.

SIR ANDREW.   I, 'tis strong, and it does indifferent well in a
 dunne colour'd stocke. Shall we set about some Revels?

SIR TOBY.   What shall we do else: were we not borne under
 Taurus?   120

SIR ANDREW.   Taurus? That's sides and heart.

SIR TOBY.   No sir, it is leggs and thighes: let me see thee caper.
 Ha, higher: ha, ha, excellent.

                                                        Exeunt.

⟨SCENE IV⟩

Enter VALENTINE, *and* VIOLA *in mans attire.*

VALENTINE.   If the Duke continue these favours towards you
 Cesario, you are like to be much advanc'd, he hath known you
 but three dayes, and already you are no stranger.

VIOLA.   You either feare his humour, or my negligence, that you
 call in question the continuance of his love. Is he inconstant sir,   5
 in his favours?

VALENTINE.   No beleeve me.

I. IV. 118 dunne] SISSON, *from* CAPELL'S "dun"; dam'd F; flame ROWE; *alii alia.*

Enter DUKE, CURIO, *and* ATTENDANTS.

VIOLA. I thanke you: heere comes the Count.
DUKE. Who saw *Cesario* hoa?
VIOLA. On your attendance my Lord heere.   10
DUKE. Stand you a-while aloofe.

⟨*The rest stand aside.*⟩

Cesario,
Thou knowst no lesse, but all: I have unclasp'd
To thee the booke even of my secret soule.
Therefore good youth, addresse thy gate unto her,
Be not deni'de accesse, stand at her doores,   15
And tell them, there thy fixed foot shall grow
Till thou have audience.
VIOLA. Sure my Noble Lord,
If she be so abandon'd to her sorrow
As it is spoke, she never will admit me.   20
DUKE. Be clamorous, and leape all civill bounds,
Rather then make unprofited returne.
VIOLA. Say I do speake with her (my Lord) what then?
DUKE. O then, unfold the passion of my love,
Surprize her with discourse of my deere faith;
It shall become thee well to act my woes: 25
She will attend it better in thy youth,
Then in a Nuntio's of more grave aspect.
VIOLA. I thinke not so, my Lord.
DUKE. Deere Lad, beleeve it;   30
For they shall yet belye thy happy yeeres,
That say thou art a man: *Dianas* lip
Is not more smooth, and rubious: thy small pipe
Is as the maidens organ, shrill, and sound,
And all is semblative a womans part.   35
I know thy constellation is right apt
For this affayre: some foure or five attend him,
All if you will: for I my selfe am best
When least in companie: prosper well in this,
And thou shalt live as freely as thy Lord,   40
To call his fortunes thine.

VIOLA. Ile do my best
To woe your Lady: ⟨*aside*⟩ yet a barrefull strife,
Who ere I woe, my selfe would be his wife.

Exeunt.

⟨SCENE V⟩

Enter MARIA, *and* CLOWN.

MARIA. Nay, either tell me where thou hast bin, or I will not
open my lippes so wide as a brissle may enter, in way of thy
excuse: my Lady will hang thee for thy absence.

CLOWN. Let her hang me: hee that is well hang'de in this world,
needs to feare no colours. 5

MARIA. Make that good.

CLOWN. He shall see none to feare.

MARIA. A good lenton answer: I can tell thee where that saying
was borne, of I feare no colours.

CLOWN. Where good mistris *Mary*? 10

MARIA. In the warrs, and that may you be bolde to say in your
foolerie.

CLOWN. Well, God give them wisedome that have it: and those
that are fooles, let them use their talents.

MARIA. Yet you will be hang'd for being so long absent; or to be 15
turn'd away: is not that as good as a hanging to you?

CLOWN. Many a good hanging, prevents a bad marriage: and for
turning away, let summer beare it out.

MARIA. You are resolute then?

CLOWN. Not so neyther, but I am resolv'd on two points. 20

MARIA. That if one breake, the other will hold: or if both breake,
your gaskins fall.

CLOWN. Apt in good faith, very apt: well go thy way, if sir *Toby*
would leave drinking, thou wert as witty a piece of *Eves* flesh, as
any in Illyria. 25

MARIA. Peace you rogue, no more o'that: here comes my Lady:
make your excuse wisely, you were best.

⟨*Exit.*⟩

Enter Lady OLIVIA, *with* MALVOLIO ⟨*and* ATTENDANTS⟩.

CLOWN. Wit, and't be thy will, put me into good fooling: those wits that thinke they have thee, doe very oft prove fooles: and I that am sure I lacke thee, may passe for a wise man. For what 30 saies *Quinapalus*, Better a witty foole, then a foolish wit. God blesse thee Lady.

OLIVIA. Take the foole away.

CLOWN. Do you not heare fellowes, take away the Ladie.

OLIVIA. Go too, y'are a dry foole: Ile no more of you: besides 35 you grow dis-honest.

CLOWN. Two faults Madona, that drinke and good counsell wil amend: for give the dry foole drink, then is the foole not dry: bid the dishonest man mend himself, if he mend, he is no longer dishonest; if hee cannot, let the Botcher mend him: any thing 40 that's mended, is but patch'd: vertu that transgresses, is but patcht with sinne, and sin that amends, is but patcht with vertue. If that this simple Sillogisme will serve, so: if it will not, what remedy? As there is no true Cuckold but calamity, so beauties a flower; The Lady bad take away the foole, therefore I say againe, take 45 her away.

OLIVIA. Sir, I bad them take away you.

CLOWN. Misprision in the highest degree. Lady, *Cucullus non facit monachum*: that's as much to say, as I weare not motley in my braine: good *Madona*, give mee leave to prove you a foole. 50

OLIVIA. Can you do it?

CLOWN. Dexteriously, good Madona.

OLIVIA. Make your proofe.

CLOWN. I must catechize you for it Madona, Good my Mouse of vertue answer mee. 55

OLIVIA. Well sir, for want of other idlenesse, Ile bide your proofe.

CLOWN. Good Madona, why mournst thou?

OLIVIA. Good foole, for my brothers death.

CLOWN. I thinke his soule is in hell, Madona.

OLIVIA. I know his soule is in heaven, foole. 60

CLOWN. The more foole (Madona) to mourne for your Brothers soule, being in heaven. Take away the Foole, Gentlemen.

OLIVIA. What thinke you of this foole *Malvolio*, doth he not mend?

MALVOLIO. Yes, and shall do, till the pangs of death shake him: 65 Infirmity that decaies the wise, doth ever make the better foole.

CLOWN.   God send you sir, a speedie Infirmity, for the better
increasing your folly: Sir *Toby* will be sworn that I am no Fox,
but he wil not passe his word for two pence that you are no Foole.

OLIVIA.   How say you to that *Malvolio*?   70

MALVOLIO.   I marvell your Ladyship takes delight in such a barren rascall: I saw him put down the other day, with an ordinary
foole, that has no more braine then a stone. Looke you now, he's
out of his gard already: unles you laugh and minister occasion to
him, he is gag'd. I protest I take these Wisemen, that crow so at   75
these set kinde of fooles, no better then the fooles Zanies.

OLIVIA.   O you are sicke of selfe-love *Malvolio*, and taste with a
distemper'd appetite. To be generous, guiltlesse, and of free disposition, is to take those things for Bird-bolts, that you deeme
Cannon bullets: There is no slander in an allow'd foole, though   80
he do nothing but rayle; nor no rayling, in a knowne discreet
man, though hee do nothing but reprove.

CLOWN.   Now Mercury indue thee with leasing, for thou speak'st
well of fooles.

Enter MARIA.

MARIA.   Madam, there is at the gate, a young Gentleman, much   85
desires to speake with you.

OLIVIA.   From the Count *Orsino*, is it?

MARIA.   I know not (Madam) 'tis a faire young man, and well
attended.

OLIVIA.   Who of my people hold him in delay?   90

MARIA.   Sir *Toby* Madam, your kinsman.

OLIVIA.   Fetch him off I pray you, he speakes nothing but madman: Fie on him. ⟨*Exit* MARIA.⟩ Go you *Malvolio*; If it be a
suit from the Count, I am sicke, or not at home. What you will,
to dismisse it. [*Exit* MALVOLIO.] Now you see sir, how your   95
fooling growes old, and people dislike it.

CLOWN.   Thou has spoke for us (Madona) as if thy eldest sonne
should be a foole: whose scull, Jove cramme with braines, for
heere he comes, one of thy kin has a most weake *Pia-mater*.

Enter SIR TOBY.

OLIVIA.   By mine honor halfe drunke. What is he at the gate   100
Cosin?

SIR TOBY.   A Gentleman.

OLIVIA.   A Gentleman? What Gentleman?

SIR TOBY.   'Tis a Gentleman heere. A plague o'these pickle her-
ring: How now Sot.   105

CLOWN.   Good Sir *Toby*.

OLIVIA.   Cosin, Cosin, how have you come so earely by this
Lethargie?

SIR TOBY.   Letcherie, I defie Letchery: there's one at the gate.

OLIVIA.   I marry, what is he?   110

SIR TOBY.   Let him be the divell and he will, I care not: give me
faith say I. Well, it's all one.

                                                            Exit.

OLIVIA.   What's a drunken man like, foole?

CLOWN.   Like a drown'd man, a foole, and a madde man: One
draught above heate, makes him a foole, the second maddes him, 115
and a third drownes him.

OLIVIA.   Go thou and seeke the Crowner, and let him sitte o'my
Coz: for he's in the third degree of drinke: hee's drown'd: go
looke after him.

CLOWN.   He is but mad yet Madona, and the foole shall looke to 120
the madman.

                                                        ⟨*Exit.*⟩

Enter MALVOLIO.

MALVOLIO.   Madam, yond young fellow sweares hee will speake
with you. I told him you were sicke, he takes on him to understand so much, and therefore comes to speak with you. I told him
you were asleepe, he seems to have a fore knowledge of that too, 125
and therefore comes to speake with you. What is to be said to
him Ladie, hee's fortified against any deniall.

OLIVIA.   Tell him, he shall not speake with me.

MALVOLIO.   Ha's beene told so: and hee sayes hee'l stand at your
doore like a Sheriffes post, and be the supporter to a bench, but 130
hee'l speake with you.

OLIVIA.   What kinde o'man is he?

MALVOLIO.   Why of mankinde.

OLIVIA.   What manner of man?

MALVOLIO.   Of verie ill manner: hee'l speake with you, will you, 135
or no.

OLIVIA.   Of what personage, and yeeres is he?

MALVOLIO.   Not yet old enough for a man, nor yong enough
for a boy: as a squash is before tis a pescod, or a Codling when
tis almost an Apple: Tis with him in standing water, betweene boy   140
and man. He is verie well-favour'd, and he speakes verie shrew-
ishly: One would thinke his mothers milke were scarse out of him.

OLIVIA.   Let him approach: Call in my Gentlewoman.

MALVOLIO.   Gentlewoman, my Lady calles.

Exit.

Enter MARIA.

OLIVIA.   Give me my vaile: come throw it ore my face,   145
Wee'l once more heare *Orsinos* Embassie.

Enter VIOLA.

VIOLA.   The honorable Ladie of the house, which is she?

OLIVIA.   Speake to me, I shall answer for her: your will?

VIOLA.   Most radiant, exquisite, and unmatchable beautie.
⟨*Pauses.*⟩ I pray you tell me if this bee the Lady of the house,   150
for I never saw her. I would bee loath to cast away my speech:
for besides that it is excellently well pend, I have taken great
paines to con it. Good Beauties, let mee sustaine no scorne; I am
very comptible, even to the least sinister usage.

OLIVIA.   Whence came you sir?   155

VIOLA.   I can say little more then I have studied, and that question's out of my part. Good gentle one, give mee modest assur-
ance, if you be the Ladie of the house, that I may proceede in my
speech.

OLIVIA.   Are you a Comedian?   160

VIOLA.   No my profound heart: and yet (by the verie phangs of
malice, I sweare) I am not that I play. Are you the Ladie of the
house?

OLIVIA.   If I do not usurpe my selfe, I am.

VIOLA.   Most certaine, if you are she, you do usurp your selfe: 165
for what is yours to bestowe, is, not yours to reserve. But this is
from my Commission: I will on with my speech in your praise,
and then shew you the heart of my message.

OLIVIA.   Come to what is important in't: I forgive you the praise.

VIOLA.   Alas, I tooke great paines to studie it, and 'tis Poeticall.   170

OLIVIA.   It is the more like to be feigned, I pray you keep it in. I heard you were sawcy at my gates, and allowd your approach rather to wonder at you, then to heare you. If you be not mad, be gone: if you have reason, be breefe: 'tis not that time of Moone with me, to make one in so skipping a dialogue.   175

MARIA.   Will you hoyst sayle sir, here lies your way.

VIOLA.   No good swabber, I am to hull here a little longer. Some mollification for your Giant, sweete Ladie; tell me your minde, I am a messenger.

OLIVIA.   Sure you have some hiddeous matter to deliver, when   180 the curtesie of it is so fearefull. Speake your office.

VIOLA.   It alone concernes your eare: I bring no overture of warre, no taxation of homage; I hold the Olyffe in my hand: my words are as full of peace, as matter.

OLIVIA.   Yet you began rudely. What are you? What would you?   185

VIOLA.   The rudenesse that hath appear'd in mee, have I learn'd from my entertainment. What I am, and what I would, are as secret as maiden-head: to your eares, Divinity; to any others, prophanation.

OLIVIA.   Give us the place alone,   190 We will heare this divinitie.

⟨*Exeunt* MARIA *and* ATTENDANTS.⟩

Now sir, what is your text?

VIOLA.   Most sweet Ladie.

OLIVIA.   A comfortable doctrine, and much may bee saide of it. Where lies your Text?   195

VIOLA.   In *Orsinoes* bosome.

OLIVIA.   In his bosome? In what chapter of his bosome?

VIOLA.   To answer by the method, in the first of his hart.

OLIVIA.   O, I have read it: it is heresie. Have you no more to say?

VIOLA.   Good Madam, let me see your face.   200

OLIVIA.   Have you any Commission from your Lord, to negoti-ate with my face: you are now out of your Text: but we will draw the Curtain, and shew you the picture. ⟨*Unveils.*⟩ Looke you sir, such a one I was this present: Ist not well done?

I. V. 173 not mad] F; "mad" (MASON) *or* "but mad" (STAUNTON) *may be right.*
178–9 tell ... messenger.] *Most editors give* "tell ... minde" *to Olivia, but* F *needs no change* (= "Speak plainly, I am but a messenger.")

VIOLA.　Excellently done, if God did all.　　　　　205
OLIVIA.　'Tis in graine sir, 'twill endure winde and weather.
VIOLA.　Tis beauty truly blent, whose red and white,
　　　　Natures owne sweet, and cunning hand laid on:
　　　　Lady, you are the cruell'st shee alive,
　　　　If you will leade these graces to the grave,　　　　　210
　　　　And leave the world no copie.
OLIVIA.　O sir, I will not be so hard-hearted: I will give out divers
　　　　scedules of my beautie. It shalbe Inventoried, and every particle
　　　　and utensile labell'd to my will: As, Item two lippes indifferent
　　　　redde, Item two grey eyes, with lids to them: Item, one necke,　215
　　　　one chin, and so forth. Were you sent hither to praise me?
VIOLA.　I see you what you are, you are too proud:
　　　　But if you were the divell, you are faire:
　　　　My Lord, and master loves you: O such love
　　　　Could be but recompenc'd, though you were crown'd　　　　　220
　　　　The non-pareil of beautie.
OLIVIA.　How does he love me?
VIOLA.　With adorations, fertill teares,
　　　　With groanes that thunder love, with sighes of fire.
OLIVIA.　Your Lord does know my mind, I cannot love him,　　　225
　　　　Yet I suppose him vertuous, know him noble,
　　　　Of great estate, of fresh and stainlesse youth;
　　　　In voyces well divulg'd, free, learn'd, and valiant,
　　　　And in dimension, and the shape of nature,
　　　　A gracious person; But yet I cannot love him:　　　　　230
　　　　He might have tooke his answer long ago.
VIOLA.　If I did love you in my masters flame,
　　　　With such a suffring, such a deadly life:
　　　　In your deniall, I would finde no sence,
　　　　I would not understand it.　　　　　235
OLIVIA.　Why, what would you?
VIOLA.　Make me a willow Cabine at your gate,
　　　　And call upon my soule within the house,
　　　　Write loyall Cantons of contemned love,
　　　　And sing them lowd even in the dead of night:　　　　　240
　　　　Hallow your name to the reverberate hilles,
　　　　And make the babling Gossip of the aire,
　　　　Cry out *Olivia*: O you should not rest

Betweene the elements of ayre, and earth,
But you should pittie me.   245
OLIVIA. You might do much:
　What is your Parentage?
VIOLA.　Above my fortunes, yet my state is well:
　I am a Gentleman.
OLIVIA.　Get you to your Lord: 250
　I cannot love him: let him send no more,
　Unlesse (perchance) you come to me againe,
　To tell me how he takes it: Fare you well:
　I thanke you for your paines: spend this for mee.
VIOLA.　I am no feede poast, Lady; keepe your purse,   255
　My Master, not my selfe, lackes recompence.
　Love make his heart of flint, that you shal love,
　And let your fervour like my masters be,
　Plac'd in contempt: Farwell fayre crueltie.

Exit.

OLIVIA.　What is your Parentage?   260
　Above my fortunes, yet my state is well;
　I am a Gentleman. Ile be sworne thou art,
　Thy tongue, thy face, thy limbes, actions, and spirit,
　Do give thee five-fold blazon: not too fast: soft, soft,
　Unlesse the Master were the man. How now?   265
　Even so quickly may one catch the plague?
　Me thinkes I feele this youths perfections
　With an invisible, and subtle stealth
　To creepe in at mine eyes. Well, let it be.
　What hoa, *Malvolio.*   270

Enter MALVOLIO.

MALVOLIO.　Heere Madam, at your service.
OLIVIA.　Run after that same peevish Messenger,
　The Counties man: he left this Ring behinde him,
　Would I, or not: tell him, Ile none of it.
　Desire him not to flatter with his Lord,
　Nor hold him up with hopes, I am not for him: 275
　If that the youth will come this way to morrow,
　Ile give him reasons for't: hie thee *Malvolio.*

MALVOLIO. Madam, I will.

Exit.

OLIVIA. I do I know not what, and feare to finde   280
Mine eye too great a flatterer for my minde:
Fate, shew thy force, our selves we do not owe,
What is decreed, must be: and be this so.

⟨*Exit.*⟩

Finis, Actus primus.

ACT II

⟨SCENE I⟩

Enter ANTONIO *and* SEBASTIAN.

ANTONIO. Will you stay no longer: nor will you not that I go
with you?

SEBASTIAN. By your patience, no: my starres shine darkely over
me; the malignancie of my fate, might perhaps distemper yours;
therefore I shall crave of you your leave, that I may beare my   5
evils alone. It were a bad recompence for your love, to lay any of
them on you.

ANTONIO. Let me yet know of you, whither you are bound.

SEBASTIAN. No sooth sir: my determinate voyage is meere
extravagancie. But I perceive in you so excellent a touch of mod-   10
estie, that you will not extort from me, what I am willing to keepe
in: therefore it charges me in manners, the rather to expresse my
selfe: you must know of mee then *Antonio*, my name is *Sebastian*
(which I call'd *Rodorigo*). My father was that *Sebastian* of *Messa-*
line, whom I know you have heard of. He left behinde him, my   15
selfe, and a sister, both borne in an houre: if the Heavens had
beene pleas'd, would we had so ended. But you sir, alter'd that,
for some houre before you tooke me from the breach of the sea,
was my sister drown'd.

ANTONIO. Alas the day.   20

SEBASTIAN. A Lady sir, though it was said shee much resembled
me, was yet of many accounted beautiful: but thogh I could not
with such estimable wonder over-farre beleeve that, yet thus farre
I will boldly publish her, shee bore a minde that envy could not
but call faire: Shee is drown'd already sir with salt water, though   25
I seeme to drowne her remembrance againe with more.

ANTONIO.   Pardon me sir, your bad entertainment.

SEBASTIAN.   O good *Antonio*, forgive me your trouble.

ANTONIO.   If you will not murther me for my love, let mee be
your servant.   30

SEBASTIAN.   If you will not undo what you have done, that is kill
him, whom you have recover'd, desire it not. Fare ye well at once,
my bosome is full of kindnesse, and I am yet so neere the manners
of my mother, that upon the least occasion more, mine eyes will
tell tales of me: I am bound to the Count Orsino's Court,   35
farewell.

                                                        Exit.

ANTONIO.   The gentlenesse of all the gods go with thee:
I have many enemies in Orsino's Court,
Else would I very shortly see thee there:
But come what may, I do adore thee so,   40
That danger shall seeme sport, and I will go.

                                                        Exit.

⟨SCENE II⟩

Enter VIOLA *and* MALVOLIO, *at severall doores.*

MALVOLIO.   Were not you ev'n now, with the Countesse *Olivia*?

VIOLA.   Even now sir, on a moderate pace, I have since ariv'd but
hither.

MALVOLIO.   She returnes this Ring to you (sir): you might have
saved mee my paines, to have taken it away your selfe. She adds   5
moreover, that you should put your Lord into a desperate assur-
ance, she will none of him. And one thing more, that you be
never so hardie to come againe in his affaires, unlesse it bee to report your Lords taking of this: receive it so.

VIOLA.   She tooke the Ring of me, Ile none of it.   10

MALVOLIO.   Come sir, you peevishly threw it to her: and her will
is, it should be so return'd: If it bee worth stooping for, there it
lies, in your eye: if not, bee it his that findes it.

                                                        Exit.

VIOLA.   I left no Ring with her: what meanes this Lady?
Fortune forbid my out-side have not charm'd her: 15
She made good view of me, indeed so much,

That me thought her eyes had lost her tongue,
For she did speake in starts distractedly.
She loves me sure, the cunning of her passion
Invites me in this churlish messenger: 20
None of my Lords Ring? Why he sent her none;
I am the man, if it be so, as tis,
Poore Lady, she were better love a dreame:
Disguise, I see thou art a wickednesse,
Wherein the pregnant enemie does much.   25
How easie is it, for the proper false
In womens waxen hearts to set their formes:
Alas, our frailtie is the cause, not wee,
For such as we are made of, such we bee:
How will this fadge? My master loves her deerely,   30
And I (poore monster) fond as much on him:
And she (mistaken) seemes to dote on me:
What will become of this? As I am man,
My state is desperate for my maisters love:
As I am woman (now alas the day)   35
What thriftlesse sighes shall poore *Olivia* breath?
O time, thou must untangle this, not I,
It is too hard a knot for me t'unty.

⟨*Exit.*⟩

⟨SCENE III⟩

Enter SIR TOBY, *and* SIR ANDREW.

SIR TOBY.   Approach Sir *Andrew*: not to bee a bedde after midnight, is to be up betimes, and *Diluculo surgere*, thou know'st.

SIR ANDREW.   Nay by my troth I know not: but I know, to be
up late, is to be up late.

SIR TOBY.   A false conclusion: I hate it as an unfill'd Canne. To   5
be up after midnight, and to go to bed then is early: so that to go
to bed after midnight, is to goe to bed betimes. Does not our life
consist of the foure Elements?

SIR ANDREW.   Faith so they say, but I thinke it rather consists
of eating and drinking.   10

II. II. 29 made of,] TYRWHITT; made, if F.

SIR TOBY.   Th'art a scholler; let us therefore eate and drinke.
Marian I say, a stoope of wine.

Enter CLOWN.

SIR ANDREW.   Heere comes the foole yfaith.

CLOWN.   How now my harts: Did you never see the Picture of
we three?   15

SIR TOBY.   Welcome asse, now let's have a catch.

SIR ANDREW.   By my troth the foole has an excellent breast. I
had rather then forty shillings I had such a legge, and so sweet a
breath to sing, as the foole has. In sooth thou wast in very gracious
fooling last night, when thou spok'st of *Pigrogromitus*, of the   20
Vapians passing the Equinoctial of *Queubus*: 'twas very good
yfaith: I sent thee sixe pence for thy Lemon, hadst it?

CLOWN.   I did impeticos thy gratillity: for *Malvolios* nose is no
Whip-stocke. My Lady has a white hand, and the Mermidons are
no bottle-ale houses.   25

SIR ANDREW.   Excellent: Why this is the best fooling, when all
is done. Now a song.

SIR TOBY.   Come on, there is sixe pence for you. Let's have a
song.

SIR ANDREW.   There's a testrill of me too: if one knight give a   30
⟨. . . .⟩

CLOWN.   Would you have a love-song, or a song of good life?

SIR TOBY.   A love song, a love song.

SIR ANDREW.   I, I. I care not for good life.

CLOWN *sings*.

> *O Mistris mine where are you roming?*   35
> *O stay and heare, your true loves coming,*
> *That can sing both high and low.*
> *Trip no further prettie sweeting.*
> *Journeys end in lovers meeting,*
> *Every wise mans sonne doth know.*   40

SIR ANDREW.   Excellent good, ifaith.

SIR TOBY.   Good, good.

CLOWN.   *What is love, tis not heereafter,*
> *Present mirth, hath present laughter:*
> *What's to come, is still unsure.*   45

II. III. 30 give a] *At end of line in* F; *next line probably omitted*; give a — F2.

> *In delay there lies no plentie,*
> *Then come kisse me sweet and twentie:*
> *Youths a stuffe will not endure.*

SIR ANDREW.   A mellifluous voyce, as I am true knight.

SIR TOBY.   A contagious breath.   50

SIR ANDREW.   Very sweet, and contagious ifaith.

SIR TOBY.   To heare by the nose, it is dulcet in contagion. But
shall we make the Welkin dance indeed? Shall wee rowze the
night-Owle in a Catch, that will drawe three soules out of one
Weaver? Shall we do that?   55

SIR ANDREW.   And you love me, let's doo't: I am dogge at a
Catch.

CLOWN.   Byrlady sir, and some dogs will catch well.

SIR ANDREW.   Most certaine: Let our Catch be, *Thou Knave.*

CLOWN.   *Hold thy peace, thou Knave* knight. I shall be constrain'd   60
in't, to call thee knave, Knight.

SIR ANDREW.   'Tis not the first time I have constrained one to
call me knave. Begin foole: it begins, *Hold thy peace.*

CLOWN.   I shall never begin if I hold my peace.

SIR ANDREW.   Good ifaith: Come begin.   65

Catch sung

Enter MARIA.

MARIA.   What a catterwalling doe you keepe heere? If my Ladie
have not call'd up her Steward *Malvolio*, and bid him turne you
out of doores, never trust me.

SIR TOBY.   My Lady's a *Catayan*, we are politicians, *Malvolios*
a Peg-a-ramsie, and *Three merry men be wee.* Am not I consangui-   70
nious? Am I not of her blood: tilly vally. Ladie, *There dwelt a*
man in Babylon, Lady, Lady.

CLOWN.   Beshrew me, the knights in admirable fooling.

SIR ANDREW.   I, he do's well enough if he be dispos'd, and so
do I too: he does it with a better grace, but I do it more naturall.   75

SIR TOBY.   *O the twelfe day of December.*

MARIA.   For the love o'God peace.

Enter MALVOLIO.

MALVOLIO.   My masters are you mad? Or what are you? Have
you no wit, manners, nor honestie, but to gabble like Tinkers at

this time of night? Do yee make an Ale-house of my Ladies house,   80
that ye squeak out your Coziers Catches without any mitigation
or remorse of voice? Is there no respect of place, persons, nor
time in you?

SIR TOBY.   We did keepe time sir in our Catches. Snecke up.

MALVOLIO.   *Sir Toby*, I must be round with you. My Lady bad   85
me tell you, that though she harbors you as her kinsman, she's
nothing ally'd to your disorders. If you can separate your selfe
and your misdemeanors, you are welcome to the house: if not,
and it would please you to take leave of her, she is very willing to
bid you farewell.   90

SIR TOBY.   *Farewell deere heart, since I must needs be gone.*

MARIA.   *Nay good Sir Toby.*

CLOWN.   *His eyes do shew his dayes are almost done.*

MALVOLIO.   Is't even so?

SIR TOBY.   *But I will never dye.*   95

CLOWN.   *Sir Toby there you lye.*

MALVOLIO.   This is much credit to you.

SIR TOBY.   *Shall I bid him go?*

CLOWN.   *What and if you do?*

SIR TOBY.   *Shall I bid him go, and spare not?*   100

CLOWN.   *O no, no, no, no, you dare not.*

SIR TOBY.   ⟨*To* CLOWN⟩ Out o'tune sir, ye lye: ⟨*To* MAL-
VOLIO⟩ Art any more then a Steward? Dost thou thinke because
thou art vertuous, there shall be no more Cakes and Ale?

CLOWN.   Yes by *S*. Anne, and Ginger shall bee hotte y'th mouth   105
too.

SIR TOBY.   Th'art i'th right. Goe sir, rub your Chaine with
crums. A stope of Wine *Maria*.

MALVOLIO.   Mistris Mary, if you priz'd my Ladies favour at any
thing more then contempt, you would not give meanes for this   110
uncivill rule; she shall know of it by this hand.

                                        Exit.

MARIA.   Go shake your eares.

SIR ANDREW.   'Twere as good a deede as to drink when a mans
a hungrie, to challenge him the field, and then to breake promise
with him, and make a foole of him.   115

II. III. 91–101 Farewell . . . *not*.] F *italicises only the last few lines of the song;
probably carelessness, but perhaps indicating that the earlier lines are spoken.*

SIR TOBY. Doo't knight, Ile write thee a Challenge: or Ile deliver thy indignation to him by word of mouth.

MARIA. Sweet Sir Toby be patient for to night: Since the youth
of the Counts was to day with my Lady, she is much out of quiet.
For Monsieur Malvolio, let me alone with him: If I do not gull   120
him into an ayword, and make him a common recreation, do not
thinke I have witte enough to lye straight in my bed: I know I
can do it.

SIR TOBY. Possesse us, possesse us, tell us something of him.

MARIA. Marrie sir, sometimes he is a kinde of Puritane.   125

SIR ANDREW. O, if I thought that, Ide beate him like a dogge.

SIR TOBY. What for being a Puritan, thy exquisite reason,
deere knight?

SIR ANDREW. I have no exquisite reason for't, but I have reason
good enough.   130

MARIA. The div'll a Puritane that hee is, or any thing constantly
but a time-pleaser, an affection'd Asse, that cons State without
booke, and utters it by great swarths. The best perswaded of
himselfe: so cram'd (as he thinkes) with excellencies, that it is his
grounds of faith, that all that looke on him, love him: and on that 135
vice in him, will my revenge finde notable cause to worke.

SIR TOBY. What wilt thou do?

MARIA. I will drop in his way some obscure Epistles of love,
wherein by the colour of his beard, the shape of his legge, the
manner of his gate, the expressure of his eye, forehead, and com- 140
plection, he shall finde himselfe most feelingly personated. I can
write very like my Ladie your Neece, on a forgotten matter wee
can hardly make distinction of our hands.

SIR TOBY. Excellent, I smell a device.

SIR ANDREW. I hav't in my nose too.   145

SIR TOBY. He shall thinke by the Letters that thou wilt drop
that they come from my Neece, and that shee's in love with him.

MARIA. My purpose is indeed a horse of that colour.

SIR ANDREW. And your horse now would make him an Asse.

MARIA. Asse, I doubt not.   150

SIR ANDREW. O twill be admirable.

MARIA. Sport royall I warrant you: I know my Physicke will

II. III. 149 SIR ANDREW.] *An.* F; *many editors give the line to Toby, as too witty
for Andrew; the opening "And" may support this.*

worke with him, I will plant you two, and let the Foole make a
third, where he shall finde the Letter: observe his construction of
it: For this night to bed, and dreame on the event: Farewell.   155

Exit.

SIR TOBY.   Good night *Penthisilea.*

SIR ANDREW.   Before me she's a good wench.

SIR TOBY.   She's a beagle true bred, and one that adores me:
what o'that?

SIR ANDREW.   I was ador'd once too.   160

SIR TOBY.   Let's to bed knight: Thou hadst neede send for more
money.

SIR ANDREW.   If I cannot recover your Neece, I am a foule way
out.

SIR TOBY.   Send for money knight, if thou hast her not i'th end,   165
call me Cut.

SIR ANDREW.   If I do not, never trust me, take it how you will.

SIR TOBY.   Come, come, Ile go burne some Sacke, tis too late
to go to bed now: Come knight, come knight.

Exeunt.

⟨SCENE IV⟩

Enter DUKE, VIOLA, CURIO, *and others.*

DUKE.   Give me some Musick; Now good morow frends.
Now good *Cesario*, but that peece of song,
That old and Anticke song we heard last night;
Me thought it did releeve my passion much,
More then light ayres, and recollected termes   5
Of these most briske and giddy-paced times.
Come, but one verse.

CURIO.   He is not heere (so please your Lordshippe) that should
sing it.

DUKE.   Who was it?   10

CURIO.   *Feste* the Jester my Lord, a foole that the Ladie *Oliviaes*
Father tooke much delight in. He is about the house.

DUKE.   Seeke him out, and play the tune the while.

⟨*Exit* CURIO.⟩

Musicke playes.

Come hither Boy, if ever thou shalt love,
In the sweet pangs of it, remember me: 15
For such as I am, all true Lovers are,
Unstaid and skittish in all motions else,
Save in the constant image of the creature
That is belov'd. How dost thou like this tune?
VIOLA.   It gives a verie eccho to the seate   20
Where love is thron'd.
DUKE.   Thou dost speake masterly,
My life upon't, yong though thou art, thine eye
Hath staid upon some favour that it loves:
Hath it not boy?   25
VIOLA.   A little, by your favour.
DUKE.   What kinde of woman ist?
VIOLA.   Of your complection.
DUKE.   She is not worth thee then. What yeares ifaith?
VIOLA.   About your yeeres my Lord.   30
DUKE.   Too old by heaven: Let still the woman take
An elder then her selfe, so weares she to him;
So swayes she levell in her husbands heart:
For boy, however we do praise our selves,
Our fancies are more giddie and unfirme,   35
More longing, wavering, sooner lost and worne,
Then womens are.
VIOLA.   I thinke it well my Lord.
DUKE.   Then let thy Love be yonger then thy selfe,
Or thy affection cannot hold the bent: 40
For women are as Roses, whose faire flowre
Being once displaid, doth fall that verie howre.
VIOLA.   And so they are: alas, that they are so:
To die, even when they to perfection grow.

Enter CURIO *and* CLOWN.

DUKE.   O fellow come, the song we had last night: 45
Marke it Cesario, it is old and plaine;
The Spinsters and the Knitters in the Sun,
And the free maides that weave their thred with bones,
Do use to chaunt it: it is silly sooth,

And dallies with the innocence of love,   50
Like the old age.

CLOWN.   Are you ready Sir?

DUKE.   I prethee sing.

The Song.

⟨CLOWN.⟩   *Come away, come away death,*   55
            And in sad cypresse let me be laide.
            Fye away, fie away breath,
            I am slaine by a faire cruell maide:
                My shrowd of white, stuck all with Ew, O prepare it.
                My part of death no one so true did share it.   60

            Not a flower, not a flower sweete
            On my blacke coffin, let there be strewne:
            Not a friend, not a friend greet
            My poor corpes, where my bones shall be throwne:
                A thousand thousand sighes to save, lay me ô where   65
                Sad true lover never find my grave, to weepe there.

DUKE.   There's for thy paines.

CLOWN.   No paines sir, I take pleasure in singing sir.

DUKE.   Ile pay thy pleasure then.

CLOWN.   Truely sir, and pleasure will be paide one time, or an-   70
other.

DUKE.   Give me now leave, to leave thee.

CLOWN.   Now the melancholly God protect thee, and the Tailor
make thy doublet of changeable Taffata, for thy minde is a very
Opall. I would have men of such constancie put to Sea, that their   75
businesse might be every thing, and their intent everie where, for
that's it, that alwayes makes a good voyage of nothing. Farewell.

Exit.

DUKE.   Let all the rest give place:

⟨*Exeunt* CURIO *and the rest.*⟩

Once more *Cesario*,

Get thee to yond same soveraigne crueltie:
Tell her my love, more noble then the world,   80

II. IV. 57 *Fye away, fie*] F; ROWE'S "Fly away, fly" *has become traditional, but is
wholly unnecessary.*

Prizes not quantitie of dirtie lands:
The parts that fortune hath bestow'd upon her,
Tell her I hold as giddily as Fortune:
But 'tis that miracle, and Queene of Jems　　　　85
That nature prankes her in, attracts my soule.
VIOLA.　But if she cannot love you sir?
DUKE.　I cannot be so answer'd.
VIOLA.　Sooth but you must.
Say that some Lady, as perhappes there is,　　　　90
Hath for your love as great a pang of heart
As you have for *Olivia*: you cannot love her:
You tel her so: Must she not then be answer'd?
DUKE.　There is no womans sides
Can bide the beating of so strong a passion,　　　　95
As love doth give my heart: no womans heart
So bigge, to hold so much, they lacke retention.
Alas, their love may be call'd appetite,
No motion of the Liver, but the Pallat,
That suffers surfet, cloyment, and revolt,　　　　100
But mine is all as hungry as the Sea,
And can digest as much, make no compare
Betweene that love a woman can beare me,
And that I owe *Olivia*.
VIOLA.　I but I know—　　　　105
DUKE.　What dost thou knowe?
VIOLA.　Too well what love women to men may owe:
In faith they are as true of heart, as we.
My Father had a daughter lov'd a man
As it might be perhaps, were I a woman　　　　110
I should your Lordship.
DUKE.　And what's her history?
VIOLA.　A blanke my Lord: she never told her love,
But let concealment like a worme i'th budde
Feede on her damaske cheeke: she pin'd in thought,　　　　115
And with a greene and yellow melancholly,
She sate like Patience on a Monument,
Smiling at greefe. Was not this love indeede?
We men may say more, sweare more, but indeed
Our shewes are more then will: for still we prove　　　　120

Much in our vowes, but little in our love.

DUKE.   But di'de thy sister of her love my Boy?

VIOLA.   I am all the daughters of my Fathers house,
And all the brothers too: and yet I know not.
Sir, shall I to this Lady?   125

DUKE.   I that's the Theame,
To her in haste: give her this Jewell: say,
My love can give no place, bide no denay.

Exeunt.

⟨SCENE V⟩

Enter SIR TOBY, SIR ANDREW, and FABIAN.

SIR TOBY.   Come thy wayes Signior *Fabian.*

FABIAN.   Nay Ile come: if I loose a scruple of this sport, let me
be boyl'd to death with Melancholly.

SIR TOBY.   Wouldst thou not be glad to have the niggardly
rascally sheepe-biter, come by some notable shame?   5

FABIAN.   I would exult man: you know he brought me out o'favour with my Lady, about a Beare-baiting heere.

SIR TOBY.   To anger him wee'l have the Beare againe, and we
will foole him blacke and blew, shall we not sir *Andrew?*

SIR ANDREW.   And we do not, it is pittie of our lives.   10

Enter MARIA.

SIR TOBY.   Heere comes the little villaine: How now my Mettle
of India?

MARIA.   Get ye all three into the box tree: *Malvolio's* comming
downe this walke, he has beene yonder i'the Sunne practising
behaviour to his own shadow this halfe houre: observe him for   15
the love of Mockerie: for I know this Letter will make a con-
templative Ideot of him. Close in the name of jeasting ⟨*they hide*⟩,
lye thou there ⟨*drops letter*⟩: for heere comes the Trowt, that
must be caught with tickling.

Exit.

Enter MALVOLIO.

MALVOLIO.   'Tis but Fortune, all is fortune. *Maria* once told me   20
she did affect me, and I have heard her self come thus neere, that

should shee fancie, it should bee one of my complection. Besides
she uses me with more a exalted respect, then any one else that
followes her. What should I thinke on't?

SIR TOBY.   Heere's an over-weening rogue.   25

FABIAN.   Oh peace: Contemplation makes a rare Turkey Cocke
of him, how he jets under his advanc'd plumes.

SIR ANDREW.   Slight I could so beate the Rogue.

SIR TOBY.   Peace I say.

MALVOLIO.   To be Count *Malvolio*.   30

SIR TOBY.   Ah Rogue.

SIR ANDREW.   Pistoll him, pistoll him.

SIR TOBY.   Peace, peace.

MALVOLIO.   There is example for't: The Lady of the *Strachy*,
married the yeoman of the wardrobe.   35

SIR ANDREW.   Fie on him Jezabel.

FABIAN.   O peace, now he's deepely in: looke how imagination
blowes him.

MALVOLIO.   Having beene three moneths married to her, sitting
in my state.   40

SIR TOBY.   O for a stone-bow to hit him in the eye.

MALVOLIO.   Calling my Officers about me, in my branch'd Vel-
vet gowne: having come from a day bedde, where I have left
Olivia sleeping.

SIR TOBY.   Fire and Brimstone.   45

FABIAN.   O peace, peace.

MALVOLIO.   And then to have the humor of state: and after a
demure travaile of regard: telling them I knowe my place, as I
would they should doe theirs: to aske for my kinsman *Toby*.

SIR TOBY.   Boltes and shackles.   50

FABIAN.   Oh peace, peace, peace, now, now.

MALVOLIO.   Seaven of my people with an obedient start, make
out for him: I frowne the while, and perchance winde up my
watch, or play with my—some rich Jewell: *Toby* approaches;
curtsies there to me.   55

SIR TOBY.   Shall this fellow live?

II. v. 29, 33 Peace. ... peace.] F; D.W., *following* WRIGHT, *assigns these lines to Fabian as peace-maker.*
54 my — some] COLLIER; my some F, F2; some F3, F4. *A neat emendation; Malvolio is about to say* "chain", *then remembers he is a gentleman.*

FABIAN. Though our silence be drawne from us with cars, yet peace.

MALVOLIO. I extend my hand to him thus: quenching my familiar smile with an austere regard of controll.   60

SIR TOBY. And do's not *Toby* take you a blow o'the lippes, then?

MALVOLIO. Saying, Cosine *Toby*, my Fortunes having cast me on your Neece, give me this prerogative of speech.

SIR TOBY. What, what?

MALVOLIO. You must amend your drunkennesse.   65

SIR TOBY. Out scab.

FABIAN. Nay patience, or we breake the sinewes of our plot.

MALVOLIO. Besides you waste the treasure of your time, with a foolish knight.

SIR ANDREW. That's mee I warrant you.   70

MALVOLIO. One sir *Andrew*.

SIR ANDREW. I knew 'twas I, for many do call mee foole.

MALVOLIO ⟨*sees letter*⟩. What employment have we heere?

FABIAN. Now is the Woodcocke neere the gin.

SIR TOBY. Oh peace, and the spirit of humors intimate reading   75
aloud to him.

MALVOLIO. By my life this is my Ladies hand: these bee her very *C's*, her *U's*, and her *T's*, and thus makes shee her great *P's*. It is in contempt of question her hand.

SIR ANDREW. Her *C's*, her *U's*, and her *T's*: why that?   80

MALVOLIO. *To the unknowne belov'd, this, and my good Wishes*: Her very Phrases: By your leave wax. Soft, and the impressure her *Lucrece*, with which she uses to seale: tis my Lady: To whom should this be?

FABIAN. This winnes him, Liver and all.   85

MALVOLIO. *Jove knowes I love, but who, Lips do not moove, no man must know.* No man must know. What followes? The numbers alter'd: No man must know, If this should be thee *Malvolio*?

SIR TOBY. Marrie hang thee brocke.   90

MALVOLIO. *I may command where I adore, but silence like a Lucresse knife:*
With bloodlesse stroke my heart doth gore, M.O.A.I. doth sway my life.

FABIAN. A fustian riddle.   95

SIR TOBY.   Excellent Wench, say I.

MALVOLIO.   *M.O.A.I.* doth sway my life. Nay but first let me
see, let me see, let me see.

FABIAN.   What dish a poyson has she drest him?

SIR TOBY.   And with what wing the stallion checkes at it?   100

MALVOLIO.   *I may command, where I adore*: Why shee may command me: I serve her, she is my Ladie. Why this is evident to any
formall capacitie. There is no obstruction in this, and the end:
What should that Alphabeticall position portend, if I could make
that resemble something in me? Softly, *M.O.A.I.*   105

SIR TOBY.   O I, make up that, he is now at a cold sent.

FABIAN.   Sowter will cry upon't for all this, though it bee as ranke
as a Fox.

MALVOLIO.   *M. Malvolio, M.* why that begins my name.

FABIAN.   Did not I say he would worke it out, the Curre is excel-   110
lent at faults.

MALVOLIO.   *M.* But then there is no consonancy in the sequell,
that suffers under probation: *A.* should follow, but *O.* does.

FABIAN.   And *O* shall end, I hope.

SIR TOBY.   I, or Ile cudgell him, and make him cry *O.*   115

MALVOLIO.   And then *I.* comes behind.

FABIAN.   I, and you had any eye behinde you, you might see
more detraction at your heeles, then Fortunes before you.

MALVOLIO.   *M, O, A, I.* This simulation is not as the former:
and yet to crush this a little, it would bow to mee, for every one   120
of these Letters are in my name. Soft, here followes prose: *If this
fall into thy hand, revolve.* In my stars I am above thee, but be not
affraid of greatnesse: Some are borne great, some atcheeve greatnesse, and some have greatnesse thrust uppon em. Thy fates open
theyr hands, let thy blood and spirit embrace them, and to inure   125
thy selfe to what thou art like to be, cast thy humble slough, and
appeare fresh. Be opposite with a kinsman, surly with servants:
Let thy tongue tang arguments of state; put thy selfe into the
tricke of singularitie. Shee thus advises thee, that sighes for thee.
Remember who commended thy yellow stockings, and wish'd to   130
see thee ever crosse garter'd: I say remember, goe too, thou art

---

II. v. 100 stallion] F; staniel (= kestrel) HANMER. F's *form may be a dialect variant
of this, and keeps the sexual implications.*

made if thou desir'st to be so: If not, let me see thee a steward still, the fellow of servants, and not woorthie to touch Fortunes fingers. Farewell, Shee that would alter services with thee, the fortunate unhappy. Daylight and champian discovers not more: This is 135 open, I will bee proud, I will reade politicke Authours, I will baffle Sir *Toby*, I will wash off grosse acquaintance, I will be point devise, the very man. I do not now foole my selfe, to let imagination jade mee; for every reason excites to this, that my Lady loves me. She did commend my yellow stockings of late, 140 shee did praise my legge being crosse-garter'd, and in this she manifests her selfe to my love, and with a kinde of injunction drives mee to these habites of her liking. I thanke my starres, I am happy: I will bee strange, stout, in yellow stockings, and crosse garter'd, even with the swiftnesse of putting on. Jove, 145 and my starres be praised. Heere is yet a postscript. *Thou canst not choose but know who I am. If thou entertainst my love, let it appeare in thy smiling, thy smiles become thee well. Therefore in my presence still smile, deere my sweete, I prethee.* Jove I thanke thee, I will smile, I wil do every thing that thou wilt have me. 150

> *Exit.*
> ⟨*The others come from hiding.*⟩

FABIAN.   I will not give my part of this sport for a pension of
   thousands to be paid from the Sophy.
SIR TOBY.   I could marry this wench for this device.
SIR ANDREW.   So could I too.
SIR TOBY.   And aske no other dowry with her, but such another 155
   jest.

Enter MARIA.

SIR ANDREW.   Nor I neither.
FABIAN.   Heere comes my noble gull catcher.
SIR TOBY.   Wilt thou set thy foote o'my necke?
SIR ANDREW.   Or o'mine either?   160
SIR TOBY.   Shall I play my freedome at tray-trip, and becom
   thy bondslave?
SIR ANDREW.   Ifaith, or I either?
SIR TOBY.   Why, thou hast put him in such a dreame, that when
   the image of it leaves him, he must run mad.   165

MARIA.   Nay but say true, do's it worke upon him?

SIR TOBY.   Like Aqua vite with a Midwife.

MARIA.   If you will then see the fruites of the sport, mark his
first approach before my Lady: hee will come to her in yellow
stockings, and 'tis a colour she abhorres, and crosse garter'd, a   170
fashion shee detests: and hee will smile upon her, which will
now be so unsuteable to her disposition, being addicted to a melancholly, as shee is, that it cannot but turn him into a notable
contempt: if you wil see it follow me.

SIR TOBY.   To the gates of Tartar, thou most excellent divell   175
of wit.

SIR ANDREW.   Ile make one too.

Exeunt.

Finis Actus secundus

ACT III

⟨SCENE I⟩

Enter VIOLA *and* CLOWN ⟨*playing on his Tabor*⟩.

VIOLA.   Save thee Friend and thy Musick: dost thou live by thy
Tabor?

CLOWN.   No sir, I live by the Church.

VIOLA.   Art thou a Churchman?

CLOWN.   No such matter sir, I do live by the Church: For, I do   5
live at my house, and my house dooth stand by the Church.

VIOLA.   So thou maist say the King lyes by a begger, if a begger
dwell neer him: or the Church stands by thy Tabor, if thy Tabor
stand by the Church.

CLOWN.   You have said sir: To see this age: A sentence is but a   10
chev'rill glove to a good witte, how quickely the wrong side may
be turn'd outward.

VIOLA.   Nay that's certaine: they that dally nicely with words,
may quickely make them wanton.

CLOWN.   I would therefore my sister had had no name Sir.   15

VIOLA.   Why man?

CLOWN.   Why sir, her names a word, and to dallie with that

word, might make my sister wanton: But indeede, words are very
Rascals, since bonds disgrac'd them.

VIOLA.   Thy reason man?   20

CLOWN.   Troth sir, I can yeeld you none without wordes, and
wordes are growne so false, I am loath to prove reason with them.

VIOLA.   I warrant thou art a merry fellow, and car'st for nothing.

CLOWN.   Not so sir, I do care for something: but in my con-
science sir, I do not care for you: if that be to care for nothing   25
sir, I would it would make you invisible.

VIOLA.   Art thou not the Lady *Olivia's* foole?

CLOWN.   No indeed sir, the Lady *Olivia* has no folly, shee will
keepe no foole sir, till she be married, and fooles are as like husbands, as Pilchers are to Herrings, the Husbands the bigger, I am   30
indeede not her foole, but hir corrupter of words.

VIOLA.   I saw thee late at the Count *Orsino's*.

CLOWN.   Foolery sir, does walke about the Orbe like the Sun, it
shines every where. I would be sorry sir, but the Foole should be
as oft with your Master, as with my Mistris: I thinke I saw your   35
wisedome there.

VIOLA.   Nay, and thou passe upon me, Ile no more with thee.
Hold there's expences for thee. ⟨*Gives him a coin.*⟩

CLOWN.   Now Jove in his next commodity of hayre, send thee a
beard.   40

VIOLA.   By my troth Ile tell thee, I am almost sicke for one,
⟨*aside*⟩ though I would not have it growe on my chinne. Is thy
Lady within?

CLOWN.   ⟨*looking at coin*⟩ Would not a paire of these have bred
sir?   45

VIOLA.   Yes being kept together, and put to use.

CLOWN.   I would play Lord *Pandarus* of *Phrygia* sir, to bring a
Cressida to this *Troylus*.

VIOLA.   I understand you sir, tis well begg'd. ⟨*Gives another coin.*⟩

CLOWN.   The matter I hope is not great sir; begging, but a begger: 50
Cressida was a begger. My Lady is within sir. I will conster to
them whence you come; who you are, and what you would are
out of my welkin, I might say Element, but the word is over-
worne.

                                                              Exit.

VIOLA.   This fellow is wise enough to play the foole,   55

And to do that well, craves a kinde of wit:
He must observe their mood on whom he jests,
The quality of persons, and the time:
And like the Haggard, checke at every Feather
That comes before his eye. This is a practice,   60
As full of labour as a Wise-mans Art:
For folly that he wisely shewes, is fit;
But wisemen folly-falne, quite taint their wit.

Enter SIR TOBY *and* SIR ANDREW.

SIR TOBY.   Save you Gentleman.
VIOLA.   And you sir.   65
SIR ANDREW.   *Dieu vou guard Monsieur.*
VIOLA.   *Et vouz ousie; vostre serviture.*
SIR ANDREW.   I hope sir, you are, and I am yours.
SIR TOBY.   Will you incounter the house, my Neece is desirous
you should enter, if your trade be to her.   70
VIOLA.   I am bound to your Neece sir, I meane she is the list of
my voyage.
SIR TOBY.   Taste your legges sir, put them to motion.
VIOLA.   My legges do better understand me sir, then I under-
stand what you meane by bidding me taste my legs.   75
SIR TOBY.   I meane to go sir, to enter.
VIOLA.   I will answer you with gate and entrance, but we are
prevented.

Enter OLIVIA, *and* ⟨MARIA⟩.

Most excellent accomplish'd Lady, the heavens raine Odours on
you.   80
SIR ANDREW.   That youth's a rare Courtier, raine odours, wel.
VIOLA.   My matter hath no voice Lady, but to your owne most
pregnant and vouchsafed eare.
SIR ANDREW.   Odours, pregnant, and vouchsafed: Ile get 'em
all three already.   85
OLIVIA.   Let the Garden doore be shut, and leave mee to my
hearing. ⟨*Exeunt* SIR TOBY, SIR ANDREW, *and* MARIA.⟩
Give me your hand sir.
VIOLA.   My dutie Madam, and most humble service.
OLIVIA.   What is your name?   90
VIOLA.   *Cesario* is your servants name, faire Princesse.

OLIVIA.   My servant sir? 'Twas never merry world,
Since lowly feigning was call'd complement:
Y'are servant to the Count *Orsino* youth.

VIOLA.   And he is yours, and his must needs be yours: 95
Your servants servant, is your servant Madam.

OLIVIA.   For him, I thinke not on him: for his thoughts,
Would they were blankes, rather then fill'd with me.

VIOLA.   Madam, I come to whet your gentle thoughts
On his behalfe.   100

OLIVIA.   O by your leave I pray you.
I bad you never speake againe of him;
But would you undertake another suite
I had rather heare you, to solicit that,
Then Musicke from the spheares.   105

VIOLA.   Deere Lady.

OLIVIA.   Give me leave, beseech you: I did send,
After the last enchantment you did here,
A Ring in chace of you. So did I abuse
My selfe, my servant, and I feare me you: 110
Under your hard construction must I sit,
To force that on you in a shamefull cunning
Which you knew none of yours. What might you think?
Have you not set mine Honor at the stake,
And baited it with all th'unmuzled thoughts   115
That tyrannous heart can think? To one of your receiving
Enough is shewne, a Cipresse, not a bosome,
Hides my heart: so let me heare you speake.

VIOLA.   I pittie you.

OLIVIA.   That's a degree to love.   120

VIOLA.   No not a grize: for tis a vulgar proofe
That verie oft we pitty enemies.

OLIVIA.   Why then me thinkes 'tis time to smile agen:
O world, how apt the poore are to be proud?
If one should be a prey, how much the better   125
To fall before the Lion, then the Wolf?

Clocke strikes.

The clocke upbraides me with the waste of time:
Be not affraid good youth, I will not have you,
And yet when wit and youth is come to harvest,

Your wife is like to reape a proper man: 130
There lies your way, due West.
VIOLA.   Then Westward hoe:
Grace and good disposition attend your Ladyship:
You'l nothing Madam to my Lord, by me?
OLIVIA.   Stay: I prethee tell me what thou thinkst of me?   135
VIOLA.   That you do thinke you are not what you are.
OLIVIA.   If I thinke so, I thinke the same of you.
VIOLA.   Then thinke you right: I am not what I am.
OLIVIA.   I would you were, as I would have you be.
VIOLA.   Would it be better Madam, then I am?   140
I wish it might, for now I am your foole.
OLIVIA.   O what a deale of scorne, lookes beautifull,
In the contempt and anger of his lip?
A murdrous guilt shewes not it selfe more soone,
Then love that would seeme hid: Loves night, is noone.   145
Cesario, by the Roses of the Spring,
By maid-hood, honor, truth, and every thing,
I love thee so, that maugre all thy pride,
Nor wit, nor reason, can my passion hide:
Do not extort thy reasons from this clause,   150
For that I woo, thou therefore hast no cause:
But rather reason thus, with reason fetter;
Love sought, is good: but given unsought, is better.
VIOLA.   By innocence I sweare, and by my youth,
I have one heart, one bosome, and one truth,   155
And that no woman has, nor never none
Shall mistris be of it, save I alone.
And so adieu good Madam, never more,
Will I my Masters teares to you deplore.
OLIVIA.   Yet come againe: for thou perhaps mayst move   160
That heart which now abhorres, to like his love.

Exeunt.

⟨SCENE II⟩

Enter SIR TOBY, SIR ANDREW, *and* FABIAN.

SIR ANDREW.   No faith, Ile not stay a jot longer.
SIR TOBY.   Thy reason deere venom, give thy reason.

FABIAN.   You must needes yeelde your reason, Sir *Andrew*?

SIR ANDREW.   Marry I saw your Neece do more favours to the
Counts Serving-man, then ever she bestow'd upon mee: I saw't   5
i'th Orchard.

SIR TOBY.   Did she see thee the while, old boy, tell me that?

SIR ANDREW.   As plaine as I see you now.

FABIAN.   This was a great argument of love in her toward you.

SIR ANDREW.   S'light; will you make an Asse o'me?   10

FABIAN.   I will prove it legitimate sir, upon the Oathes of judge-
ment, and reason.

SIR TOBY.   And they have beene grand Jurie men, since before
Noah was a Saylor.

FABIAN.   Shee did shew favour to the youth in your sight, onely   15
to exasperate you, to awake your dormouse valour, to put fire in
your Heart, and brimstone in your Liver: you should then have
accosted her, and with some excellent jests, fire-new from the
mint, you should have bangd the youth into dumbenesse: this
was look'd for at your hand, and this was baulkt: the double gilt   20
of this opportunitie you let time wash off, and you are now sayld
into the North of my Ladies opinion, where you will hang like
an ysickle on a Dutchmans beard, unlesse you do redeeme it, by
some laudable attempt, either of valour or policie.

SIR ANDREW.   And't be any way, it must be with Valour, for   25
policie I hate: I had as liefe be a Brownist, as a Politician.

SIR TOBY.   Why then build me thy fortunes upon the basis of
valour. Challenge me the Counts youth to fight with him, hurt
him in eleven places, my Neece shall take note of it, and assure
thy selfe, there is no love-Broker in the world, can more prevaile   30
in mans commendation with woman, then report of valour.

FABIAN.   There is no way but this sir *Andrew*.

SIR ANDREW.   Will either of you beare me a challenge to him?

SIR TOBY.   Go, write it in a martial hand, be curst and briefe:
it is no matter how wittie, so it bee eloquent, and full of inven-   35
tion: taunt him with the license of Inke: if thou thou'st him
some thrice, it shall not be amisse, and as many Lyes, as will lye
in thy sheete of paper, although the sheete were bigge enough
for the bedde of *Ware* in England, set 'em downe, go, about it.
Let there bee gaulle enough in thy inke, though thou write with   40
a Goose-pen, no matter: about it.

SIR ANDREW.　Where shall I finde you?

SIR TOBY.　Wee'l call thee at the Cubiculo: Go.

　　　　　　　　　　　　　Exit SIR ANDREW.

FABIAN.　This is a deere Manakin to you Sir *Toby*.

SIR TOBY.　I have beene deere to him lad, some two thousand　45
strong, or so.

FABIAN.　We shall have a rare Letter from him; but you'le not
deliver't.

SIR TOBY.　Never trust me then: and by all meanes stirre on the
youth to an answer. I thinke Oxen and waine-ropes cannot hale　50
them together. For *Andrew*, if he were open'd and you finde so
much blood in his Liver, as will clog the foote of a flea, Ile eate
the rest of th'anatomy.

FABIAN.　And his opposit the youth beares in his visage no great
presage of cruelty.　　　　　　　　　　　　　　　55

Enter MARIA.

SIR TOBY.　Looke where the youngest Wren of mine comes.

MARIA.　If you desire the spleene, and will laughe your selves
into stitches, follow me; yond gull *Malvolio* is turned Heathen,
a verie Renegatho; for there is no christian that meanes to be　60
saved by beleeving rightly, can ever beleeve such impossible passages of grossenesse. Hee's in yellow stockings.

SIR TOBY.　And crosse garter'd?

MARIA.　Most villanously: like a Pedant that keepes a Schoole i'th
Church: I have dogg'd him like his murtherer. He does obey every　65
point of the Letter that I dropt, to betray him: He does smile his
face into more lynes, then is in the new Mappe, with the augmentation of the Indies: you have not seene such a thing as tis: I
can hardly forbeare hurling things at him, I know my Ladie will
strike him: if shee doe, hee'l smile, and take't for a great favour.　70

SIR TOBY.　Come bring us, bring us where he is.

　　　　　　　　　　　　　Exeunt Omnes.

⟨SCENE III⟩

Enter SEBASTIAN *and* ANTONIO.

SEBASTIAN.　I would not by my will have troubled you,
But since you make your pleasure of your paines,
I will no further chide you.

ANTONIO.   I could not stay behinde you: my desire
    (More sharpe then filed steele) did spurre me forth,   5
    And not all love to see you (though so much
    As might have drawne one to a longer voyage)
    But jealousie, what might befall your travell,
    Being skillesse in these parts: which to a stranger,
    Unguided, and unfriended, often prove   10
    Rough, and unhospitable. My willing love,
    The rather by these arguments of feare,
    Set forth in your pursuite.
SEBASTIAN.   My kinde *Anthonio,*
    I can no other answer make, but thankes,   15
    And thankes, and ever thankes: and oft good turnes,
    Are shuffel'd off with such uncurrant pay:
    But were my worth, as is my conscience firme,
    You should finde better dealing: what's to do?
    Shall we go see the reliques of this Towne?   20
ANTONIO.   To morrow sir, best first go see your Lodging.
SEBASTIAN.   I am not weary, and 'tis long to night,
    I pray you let us satisfie our eyes
    With the memorials, and the things of fame
    That do renowne this City.   25
ANTONIO.   Would youl'd pardon me:
    I do not without danger walke these streetes.
    Once in a sea-fight 'gainst the Count his gallies,
    I did some service, of such note indeede,
    That were I tane heere, it would scarse be answer'd.   30
SEBASTIAN.   Belike you slew great number of his people.
ANTIONIO.   Th offence is not of such a bloody nature,
    Albeit the quality of the time, and quarrell
    Might well have given us bloody argument:
    It might have since bene answer'd in repaying   35
    What we tooke from them, which for Traffiques sake
    Most of our City did. Onely my selfe stood out,
    For which if I be lapsed in this place
    I shall pay deere.
SEBASTIAN.   Do not then walke too open.   40

III. III. 16 And ... oft] And thanks, and ever thanks; and oft THEOBALD; And
thankes: and euer oft F; ll. 16–17 *om.* F2, 3, 4; *no conjecture is wholly satisfactory.*

ANTONIO.　It doth not fit me: hold sir, here's my purse,
　In the South Suburbes at the Elephant
　Is best to lodge: I will bespeake our dyet,
　Whiles you beguile the time, and feed your knowledge
　With viewing of the Towne, there shall you have me.　45
SEBASTIAN.　Why I your purse?
ANTONIO.　Haply your eye shall light upon some toy
　You have desire to purchase: and your store
　I thinke is not for idle Markets, sir.
SEBASTIAN.　Ile be your purse-bearer, and leave you for an houre.　50
ANTONIO.　To th'Elephant.
SEBASTIAN.　I do remember.

Exeunt.

⟨SCENE IV⟩

Enter OLIVIA *and* MARIA.

OLIVIA.　⟨*to herself*⟩ I have sent after him, he sayes hee'l come:
　How shall I feast him? What bestow of him?
　For youth is bought more oft, then begg'd, or borrow'd.
　I speake too loud:
　　　⟨*To* MARIA⟩ Where's *Malvolio*, he is sad, and civill,
　And suites well for a servant with my fortunes,　5
　Where is *Malvolio*?
MARIA.　He's comming Madame: but in very strange manner. He
　is sure possest Madam.
OLIVIA.　Why what's the matter, does he rave?
MARIA.　No Madam, he does nothing but smile: your Ladyship　10
　were best to have some guard about you, if hee come, for sure
　the man is tainted in's wits.
OLIVIA.　Go call him hither.

⟨*Exit* MARIA.⟩

　　　I am as madde as hee,
　If sad and merry madnesse equall bee.　15

Enter ⟨MARIA *and*⟩ MALVOLIO.
　How now *Malvolio*?
MALVOLIO.　Sweet Lady, ho, ho.

OLIVIA. Smil'st thou? I sent for thee upon a sad occasion.

MALVOLIO. Sad, Lady, I could be sad: this does make some
obstruction in the blood: this crosse-gartering, but what of that? 20
If it please the eye of one, it is with me as the very true Sonnet is:
Please one, and please all.

OLIVIA. Why how doest thou man?
What is the matter with thee?

MALVOLIO. Not blacke in my minde, though yellow in my 25
legges: It did come to his hands, and Commaunds shall be exe-
cuted. I thinke we doe know the sweet Romane hand.

OLIVIA. Wilt thou go to bed Malvolio?

MALVOLIO. To bed? I sweet heart, and Ile come to thee.

OLIVIA. God comfort thee: Why dost thou smile so, and kisse 30
thy hand so oft?

MARIA. How do you Malvolio?

MALVOLIO. At your request:
Yes Nightingales answere Dawes.

MARIA. Why appeare you with this ridiculous boldnesse before 35
my Lady?

MALVOLIO. Be not afraid of greatnesse: 'twas well writ.

OLIVIA. What meanst thou by that Malvolio?

MALVOLIO. Some are borne great.

OLIVIA. Ha? 40

MALVOLIO. Some atcheeve greatnesse.

OLIVIA. What sayst thou?

MALVOLIO. And some have greatnesse thrust upon them.

OLIVIA. Heaven restore thee.

MALVOLIO. Remember who commended thy yellow stockings. 45

OLIVIA. Thy yellow stockings?

MALVOLIO. And wish'd to see thee crosse garter'd.

OLIVIA. Crosse garter'd?

MALVOLIO. Go too, thou art made, if thou desir'st to be so.

OLIVIA. Am I made? 50

MALVOLIO. If not, let me see thee a servant still.

OLIVIA. Why this is verie Midsommer madnesse.

Enter SERVANT.

III. IV. 23 OLIVIA] *Ol.* F2; *Mal.* F; *Mar.* COLLIER. *Perhaps* l. 23 *should be
given to Maria, and* l. 24 *to Olivia.*

SERVANT. Madame, the young Gentleman of the Count *Orsino's*
is return'd, I could hardly entreate him backe: he attends your
Ladyships pleasure.   55
OLIVIA. Ile come to him. ⟨*Exit* SERVANT.⟩ Good *Maria*, let
this fellow be look'd too. Where's my Cosine *Toby*, let some of
my people have a speciall care of him, I would not have him mis-
carrie for the halfe of my Dowry.

Exit ⟨OLIVIA *and* MARIA.⟩

MALVOLIO. Oh ho, do you come neere me now: no worse man   60
then sir *Toby* to looke to me. This concurres directly with the
Letter, she sends him on purpose, that I may appeare stubborne
to him: for she incites me to that in the Letter. Cast thy humble
slough sayes she: be opposite with a Kinsman, surly with servants, let thy tongue tang arguments of state, put thy selfe into the 65
tricke of singularity: and consequently setts downe the manner
how: as a sad face, a reverend carriage, a slow tongue, in the habite
of some Sir of note, and so foorth. I have lymde her, but it is
Joves doing, and Jove make me thankefull. And when she went
away now, let this Fellow be look'd too: Fellow? not *Malvolio*, nor 70
after my degree, but Fellow. Why every thing adheres togither,
that no dramme of a scruple, no scruple of a scruple, no obstacle, no
incredulous or unsafe circumstance: What can be saide? Nothing
that can be, can come betweene me, and the full prospect of my
hopes. Well Jove, not I, is the doer of this, and he is to be thanked. 75

Enter SIR TOBY, FABIAN, and MARIA.

SIR TOBY. Which way is hee in the name of sanctity? If all the
divels of hell be drawne in little, and Legion himselfe possest
him, yet Ile speake to him.
FABIAN. Heere he is, heere he is: how ist with you sir? How ist
with you man?   80
MALVOLIO. Go off, I discard you: let me enjoy my private: go
off.
MARIA. Lo, how hollow the fiend speakes within him; did not I
tell you? Sir *Toby*, my Lady prayes you to have a care of him.
MALVOLIO. Ah ha, does she so?   85
SIR TOBY. Go too, go too: peace, peace, wee must deale gently

III. IV. 79–80 How . . . man?] F; *sometimes assigned to Toby.*

T.N.—3

with him: Let me alone. How do you *Malvolio?* How ist with you?
What man, defie the divell: consider, he's an enemy to mankinde.

MALVOLIO.   Do you know what you say?

MARIA.   La you, and you speake ill of the divell, how he takes it   90
at heart. Pray God he be not bewitch'd.

FABIAN.   Carry his water to th'wise woman.

MARIA.   Marry and it shall be done to morrow morning if I live.
My Lady would not loose him for more then ile say.

MALVOLIO.   How now mistris?   95

MARIA.   Oh Lord.

SIR TOBY.   Prethee hold thy peace, this is not the way: Doe you
not see you move him? Let me alone with him.

FABIAN.   No way but gentlenesse, gently, gently: the Fiend is
rough, and will not be roughly us'd.   100

SIR TOBY.   Why how now my bawcock? how dost thou chuck?

MALVOLIO.   Sir.

SIR TOBY.   I biddy, come with me. What man, tis not for
gravity to play at cherrie-pit with Sathan. Hang him foul Colliar.

MARIA.   Get him to say his prayers, good sir *Toby* gette him to 105
pray.

MALVOLIO.   My prayers Minx.

MARIA.   No I warrant you, he will not heare of godlynesse.

MALVOLIO.   Go hang your selves all: you are ydle shallowe
things, I am not of your element, you shall knowe more heere-   110
after.

                                                             Exit.

SIR TOBY.   Ist possible?

FABIAN.   If this were plaid upon a stage now, I could condemne
it as an improbable fiction.

SIR TOBY.   His very genius hath taken the infection of the   115
device man.

MARIA.   Nay pursue him now, least the device take ayre, and
taint.

FABIAN.   Why we shall make him mad indeede.

MARIA.   The house will be the quieter.   120

SIR TOBY.   Come, wee'l have him in a darke room and bound.
My Neece is already in the beleefe that he's mad: we may carry
it thus for our pleasure, and his pennance, til our very pastime
tyred out of breath, prompt us to have mercy on him: at which

time, we wil bring the device to the bar and crowne thee for a 125
finder of madmen: but see, but see.

Enter SIR ANDREW.

FABIAN.   More matter for a May morning.
SIR ANDREW.   Heere's the Challenge, reade it: I warrant there's
vinegar and pepper in't.
FABIAN.   Ist so sawcy?   130
SIR ANDREW.   I, ist? I warrant him: do but read.
SIR TOBY.   Give me. ⟨*Reads*⟩ *Youth, whatsoever thou art, thou*
art but a scurvy fellow.
FABIAN.   Good, and valiant.
SIR TOBY.   *Wonder not, nor admire not in thy minde why I doe call* 135
thee so, for I will shew thee no reason for't.
FABIAN.   A good note, that keepes you from the blow of the Law.
SIR TOBY.   *Thou comst to the Lady Olivia, and in my sight she*
uses thee kindly: but thou lyest in thy throat, that is not the matter
I challenge thee for.   140
FABIAN.   Very breefe, and to exceeding good sence-lesse.
SIR TOBY.   *I will way-lay thee going home, where if it be thy*
chance to kill me—
FABIAN.   Good.
SIR TOBY.   *Thou kilst me like a rogue and a villaine.*   145
FABIAN   Still you keepe o'th windie side of the Law: good.
SIR TOBY.   *Fartheewell, and God have mercie upon one of our*
soules. He may have mercie upon mine, but my hope is better, and
so looke to thy selfe. Thy friend as thou usest him, and thy sworne
enemie, Andrew Ague-cheeke.   150
If this Letter move him not, his legges cannot: Ile giv't him.
MARIA.   You may have verie fit occasion for't: he is now in some
commerce with my Ladie, and will by and by depart.
SIR TOBY.   Go sir *Andrew*: scout mee for him at the corner of the
Orchard like a bum-Baylie: so soone as ever thou seest him,   155
draw, and as thou draw'st, sweare horrible: for it comes to passe
oft, that a terrible oath, with a swaggering accent sharpely
twang'd off, gives manhoode more approbation, then ever proofe
it selfe would have earn'd him. Away.
SIR ANDREW.   Nay let me alone for swearing.   160

                                                    Exit.

SIR TOBY. Now will not I deliver his Letter: for the behaviour of the young Gentleman, gives him out to be of good capacity, and breeding: his employment betweene his Lord and my Neece, confirmes no lesse. Therefore, this Letter being so excellently ignorant, will breede no terror in the youth: he will finde it 165 comes from a Clodde-pole. But sir, I will deliver his Challenge by word of mouth; set upon *Ague-cheeke* a notable report of valor, and drive the Gentleman (as I know his youth will aptly receive it) into a most hideous opinion of his rage, skill, furie, and impetuositie. This will so fright them both, that they wil 170 kill one another by the looke, like Cockatrices.

Enter OLIVIA *and* VIOLA.

FABIAN. Heere he comes with your Neece, give them way till he take leave, and presently after him.

SIR TOBY. I wil meditate the while upon some horrid message for a Challenge. 175

⟨*Exeunt* SIR TOBY, FABIAN, *and* MARIA.⟩

OLIVIA. I have said too much unto a hart of stone,
And laid mine honour too unchary on't:
There's something in me that reproves my fault:
But such a head-strong potent fault it is,
That it but mockes reproofe. 180

VIOLA. With the same haviour that your passion beares,
Goes on my Masters greefes.

OLIVIA. Heere, weare this Jewell for me, tis my picture:
Refuse it not, it hath no tongue, to vex you:
And I beseech you come againe to morrow. 185
What shall you aske of me that Ile deny,
That honour (sav'd) may upon asking give?

VIOLA. Nothing but this, your true love for my master.

OLIVIA. How with mine honor may I give him that,
Which I have given to you? 190

VIOLA. I will acquit you.

OLIVIA. Well, come againe to morrow: far-thee-well,
A Fiend like thee might beare my soule to hell.

⟨*Exit.*⟩

Enter SIR TOBY *and* FABIAN.

SIR TOBY.　Gentleman, God save thee.

VIOLA.　And you sir.　　　　　　　　　　　　　　　195

SIR TOBY.　That defence thou hast, betake thee too't: of what
nature the wrongs are thou hast done him, I knowe not: but thy
intercepter full of despight, bloody as the Hunter, attends thee
at the Orchard end: dismount thy tucke, be yare in thy preparation, for thy assaylant is quick, skilfull, and deadly.　　　200

VIOLA.　You mistake sir I am sure, no man hath any quarrell to
me: my remembrance is very free and cleere from any image of
offence done to any man.

SIR TOBY.　You'l finde it otherwise I assure you: therefore, if
you hold your life at any price, betake you to your gard: for　205
your opposite hath in him what youth, strength, skill, and wrath,
can furnish man withall.

VIOLA.　I pray you sir what is he?

SIR TOBY.　He is knight dubb'd with unhatch'd Rapier, and on
carpet consideration, but he is a divell in private brall, soules and　210
bodies hath he divorc'd three, and his incensement at this moment
is so implacable, that satisfaction can be none, but by pangs of
death and sepulcher: Hob, nob, is his word: giv't or take't.

VIOLA.　I will returne againe into the house, and desire some
conduct of the Lady. I am no fighter, I have heard of some kinde　215
of men, that put quarrells purposely on others, to taste their valour: belike this is a man of that quirke.

SIR TOBY.　Sir, no: his indignation derives it selfe out of a very
competent injurie, therefore get you on, and give him his desire.
Backe you shall not to the house, unlesse you undertake that　220
with me, which with as much safetie you might answer him:
therefore on, or strippe your sword starke naked: for meddle you
must that's certain, or forsweare to weare iron about you.

VIOLA.　This is as uncivill as strange. I beseech you doe me this
courteous office, as to know of the Knight what my offence to　225
him is: it is something of my negligence, nothing of my purpose.

SIR TOBY.　I will doe so. Signiour *Fabian*, stay you by this
Gentleman, till my returne.

　　　　　　　　　　　　　　　　　Exit SIR TOBY.

VIOLA.　Pray you sir, do you know of this matter?

FABIAN.   I know the knight is incenst against you, even to a   230
mortall arbitrement, but nothing of the circumstance more.

VIOLA.   I beseech you what manner of man is he?

FABIAN.   Nothing of that wonderfull promise to read him by his
forme, as you are like to finde him in the proofe of his valour.
He is indeede sir, the most skilfull, bloudy, and fatall opposite   235
that you could possibly have found in anie part of Illyria: will
you walke towards him, I will make your peace with him, if I can.

VIOLA.   I shall bee much bound to you for't: I am one, that had
rather go with sir Priest, then sir knight: I care not who knowes
so much of my mettle.   240

Exeunt.

Enter SIR TOBY *and* SIR ANDREW.

SIR TOBY.   Why man hee's a verie divell, I have not seen such a
firago: I had a passe with him, rapier, scabberd, and all: and he
gives me the stucke in with such a mortall motion that it is in-
evitable: and on the answer, he payes you as surely, as your feete
hits the ground they step on. They say, he has bin Fencer to the   245
Sophy.

SIR ANDREW.   Pox on't, Ile not meddle with him.

SIR TOBY.   I but he will not now be pacified, *Fabian* can scarse
hold him yonder.

SIR ANDREW.   Plague on't, and I thought he had beene valiant,   250
and so cunning in Fence, I'de have seene him damn'd ere I'de
have challeng'd him. Let him let the matter slip, and Ile give him
my horse, gray Capilet.

SIR TOBY.   Ile make the motion: stand heere, make a good shew
on't, this shall end without the perdition of soules, ⟨*aside*⟩ marry   255
Ile ride your horse as well as I ride you.

Enter FABIAN *and* VIOLA.

⟨*To* FABIAN⟩   I have his horse to take up the quarrell, I have
perswaded him the youths a divell.

FABIAN.   He is as horribly conceited of him: and pants, and lookes
pale, as if a Beare were at his heeles.   260

SIR TOBY.   ⟨*To* VIOLA⟩ There's no remedie sir, he will fight
with you for's oath sake: marrie he hath better bethought him of
his quarrell, and hee findes that now scarse to bee worth talking

III. IV. 240 *Exeunt*.] *Some editors start a new scene here.*

of: therefore draw for the supportance of his vowe, he protests
he will not hurt you.　　　　　　　　　　　　　　　　　265

VIOLA.　Pray God defend me: a little thing would make me tell
them how much I lacke of a man.

FABIAN.　Give ground if you see him furious.

SIR TOBY.　Come sir *Andrew*, there's no remedie, the Gentleman will for his honors sake have one bowt with you: he cannot　270
by the Duello avoide it: but hee has promised me, as he is a
Gentleman and a Soldiour, he will not hurt you. Come on, too't.

SIR ANDREW.　Pray God he keepe his oath.

⟨*They draw.*⟩

Enter ANTONIO.

VIOLA.　I do assure you tis against my will.

ANTONIO.　Put up your sword: if this yong Gentleman　　275
Have done offence, I take the fault on me:
If you offend him, I for him defie you.

SIR TOBY.　You sir? Why, what are you?

ANTONIO.　One sir, that for his love dares yet do more
Then you have heard him brag to you he will.　　　　280

SIR TOBY.　Nay, if you be an undertaker, I am for you.

⟨*They draw.*⟩

Enter OFFICERS.

FABIAN.　O good sir *Toby* hold: heere come the Officers.

SIR TOBY.　⟨*To* ANTONIO⟩ Ile be with you anon.

VIOLA.　Pray sir, put your sword up if you please.

SIR ANDREW.　Marry will I sir: and for that I promis'd you Ile　285
be as good as my word. Hee will beare you easily, and raines well.

FIRST OFFICER.　This is the man, do thy Office.

SECOND OFFICER.　*Anthonio*, I arrest thee at the suit of Count
Orsino.

ANTONIO.　You do mistake me sir.

FIRST OFFICER.　No sir, no jot: I know your favour well:　　290
Though now you have no sea-cap on your head:
Take him away, he knowes I know him well.

ANTONIO.　I must obey. ⟨*To* VIOLA⟩ This comes with seeking you:
But there's no remedie, I shall answer it:
What will you do, now my necessitie　　　　　　　　　295

Makes me to aske you for my purse? It greeves mee
Much more, for what I cannot do for you,
Then what befals my selfe: you stand amaz'd,
But be of comfort.

SECOND OFFICER.   Come sir away.   300

ANTONIO.   I must entreat of you some of that money.

VIOLA.   What money sir?
For the fayre kindnesse you have shew'd me heere,
And part being prompted by your present trouble,
Out of my leane and low ability   305
Ile lend you something: my having is not much,
Ile make division of my present with you:
Hold, there's halfe my Coffer.

ANTONIO.   Will you deny me now,
Ist possible that my deserts to you   310
Can lacke perswasion? Do not tempt my misery,
Least that it make me so unsound a man
As to upbraid you with those kindnesses
That I have done for you.

VIOLA.   I know of none,   315
Nor know I you by voyce, or any feature:
I hate ingratitude more in a man,
Then lying, vainnesse, babling drunkennesse,
Or any taint of vice, whose strong corruption
Inhabites our fraile blood.   320

ANTONIO.   Oh heavens themselves.

SECOND OFFICER.   Come sir, I pray you go.

ANTONIO.   Let me speake a little. This youth that you see heere,
I snatch'd one halfe out of the jawes of death,
Releev'd him with such sanctitie of love;   325
And to his image, which me thought did promise
Most venerable worth, did I devotion.

FIRST OFFICER.   What's that to us, the time goes by: Away.

ANTONIO.   But oh, how vilde an idoll proves this God:
Thou hast *Sebastian* done good feature, shame.   330
In Nature, there's no blemish but the minde:
None can be call'd deform'd, but the unkinde.
Vertue is beauty, but the beauteous evill
Are empty trunkes, ore-flourish'd by the devill.

FIRST OFFICER. The man growes mad, away with him: 335
  Come, come sir.
ANTONIO. Leade me on.

Exit ⟨ANTONIO *with officers*⟩.

VIOLA. Me thinkes his words do from such passion flye
  That he beleeves himselfe, so do not I: 340
  Prove true imagination, oh prove true,
  That I deere brother, be now tane for you.
SIR TOBY. Come hither Knight, come hither *Fabian*: Weel
  whisper ore a couplet or two of most sage sawes.
VIOLA. He nam'd *Sebastian*: I my brother know 345
  Yet living in my glasse: even such, and so
  In favour was my Brother, and he went
  Still in this fashion, colour, ornament,
  For him I imitate: Oh if it prove,
  Tempests are kinde, and salt waves fresh in love. 350

⟨*Exit.*⟩

SIR TOBY. A very dishonest paltry boy, and more a coward
  then a Hare, his dishonesty appeares, in leaving his frend heere
  in necessity, and denying him: and for his cowardship aske
  Fabian.
FABIAN. A Coward, a most devout Coward, religious in it. 355
SIR ANDREW. Slid Ile after him againe, and beate him.
SIR TOBY. Do, cuffe him soundly, but never draw thy sword.
SIR ANDREW. And I do not—

⟨*Exit.*⟩

FABIAN. Come, let's see the event.
SIR TOBY. I dare lay any money, twill be nothing yet.

Exit ⟨*with* FABIAN.⟩

ACT IV

⟨SCENE I⟩

Enter SEBASTIAN *and* CLOWN.

CLOWN. Will you make me beleeve, that I am not sent for you?
SEBASTIAN. Go too, go too, thou art a foolish fellow,
  Let me be cleere of thee.

CLOWN.   Well held out yfaith: No, I do not know you, nor I am
not sent to you by my Lady, to bid you come speake with her: 5
nor your name is not Master *Cesario*, nor this is not my nose neyther: Nothing that is so, is so.
SEBASTIAN.   I prethee vent thy folly some-where else,
Thou know'st not me.
CLOWN.   Vent my folly: He has heard that word of some great   10
man, and now applyes it to a foole. Vent my folly: I am affraid
this great lubber the World will prove a Cockney: I prethee now
ungird thy strangenes, and tell me what I shall vent to my Lady.
Shall I vent to hir that thou art comming?
SEBASTIAN.   I prethee foolish greeke depart from me,   15
There's money for thee, if you tarry longer,
I shall give worse paiment.
CLOWN.   By my troth thou hast an open hand: these Wisemen
that give fooles money, get themselves a good report, after
foureteene yeares purchase.   20

Enter SIR ANDREW, SIR TOBY, *and* FABIAN.

SIR ANDREW.   Now sir, have I met you again: ther's for you.
⟨*Strikes* SEBASTIAN.⟩
SEBASTIAN.   ⟨*Beats him.*⟩ Why there's for thee, and there, and
there,
Are all the people mad?
SIR TOBY.   Hold sir, or Ile throw your dagger ore the house.
⟨*Seizes* SEBASTIAN.⟩
CLOWN.   This will I tell my Lady straight, I would not be in   25
some of your coats for two pence.
⟨*Exit.*⟩
SIR TOBY.   Come on sir, hold.
SIR ANDREW.   Nay let him alone, Ile go another way to worke
with him: Ile have an action of Battery against him, if there be
any law in Illyria: though I stroke him first, yet it's no matter   30
for that.
SEBASTIAN.   Let go thy hand.
SIR TOBY.   Come sir, I will not let you go. ⟨SEBASTIAN *half*

IV. I. 33 ff. SEBASTIAN ... thy sword.] *The s.ds. here follow the analysis in*
SISSON; D.W. *regards* ll. 34–5 ("Come ... flesh'd:") *as addressed ironically to Sir
Andrew.*

draws his sword.⟩ Come my yong souldier put up your yron: 35
you are well flesh'd: Come on.

SEBASTIAN.   ⟨*Breaks loose.*⟩ I will be free from thee. What
                              wouldst thou now? ⟨*Draws.*⟩
If thou dar'st tempt me further, draw thy sword.

SIR TOBY.   What, what? ⟨*Draws.*⟩ Nay then I must have an
Ounce or two of this malapert blood from you.

⟨*They fight.*⟩

Enter OLIVIA.

OLIVIA.   Hold *Toby*, on thy life I charge thee hold.   40
SIR TOBY.   Madam.
OLIVIA.   Will it be ever thus? Ungracious wretch,
Fit for the Mountaines, and the barbarous Caves,
Where manners nere were preach'd: out of my sight.
Be not offended, deere *Cesario*:   45
Rudesbey be gone.

⟨*Exeunt* SIR TOBY, SIR ANDREW, *and* FABIAN.⟩

I prethee gentle friend,
Let thy fayre wisedome, not thy passion sway
In this uncivill, and unjust extent
Against thy peace. Go with me to my house,
And heare thou there how many fruitlesse prankes   50
This Ruffian hath botch'd up, that thou thereby
Mayst smile at this: Thou shalt not choose but goe:
Do not denie, beshrew his soule for mee,
He started one poore heart of mine, in thee.

SEBASTIAN.   What rellish is in this? How runs the streame? 55
Or I am mad, or else this is a dreame:
Let fancie still my sense in Lethe steepe,
If it be thus to dreame, still let me sleepe.

OLIVIA.   Nay come I prethee, would thoud'st be ruled by me.
SEBASTIAN.   Madam, I will.   60
OLIVIA.   O say so, and so be.

Exeunt.

⟨SCENE II⟩

Enter MARIA *and* CLOWN.

MARIA.   Nay, I prethee put on this gown, and this beard, make
him beleeve thou art sir *Topas* the Curate, doe it quickly. Ile
call sir *Toby* the whilst.

⟨*Exit.*⟩

CLOWN.   Well, Ile put it on, and I will dissemble my selfe in't,
and I would I were the first that ever dissembled in such a gowne.   5
I am not tall enough to become the function well, nor leane
enough to bee thought a good Studient: but to be said an honest
man and a good houskeeper goes as fairely, as to say, a carefull
man, and a great scholler. The Competitors enter.

Enter SIR TOBY ⟨*and* MARIA⟩.

SIR TOBY.   Jove blesse thee M. Parson.   10
CLOWN.   *Bonos dies* sir *Toby*: for as the old hermit of *Prage* that
never saw pen and inke, very wittily sayd to a Neece of King
Gorbodacke, that that is, is: so I being M. Parson, am M. Parson;
for what is that, but that? and is, but is?
SIR TOBY.   To him sir *Topas*.   15
CLOWN.   What hoa, I say, Peace in this prison.
SIR TOBY.   The knave counterfets well: a good knave.

MALVOLIO ⟨*speaks*⟩ *within.*

MALVOLIO.   Who cals there?
CLOWN.   Sir *Topas* the Curate, who comes to visit *Malvolio* the
Lunaticke.   20
MALVOLIO.   Sir *Topas*, sir *Topas*, good sir *Topas* goe to my
Ladie.
CLOWN.   Out hyperbolicall fiend, how vexest thou this man?
Talkest thou nothing but of Ladies?
SIR TOBY.   Well said M. Parson.   25
MALVOLIO.   Sir *Topas*, never was man thus wronged, good sir
Topas do not thinke I am mad: they have layde mee heere in
hideous darknesse.
CLOWN.   Fye, thou dishonest Sathan: I call thee by the most

modest termes, for I am one of those gentle ones, that will use   30
the divell himselfe with curtesie: sayst thou that house is darke?

MALVOLIO.   As hell sir *Topas*.

CLOWN.   Why it hath bay Windowes transparant as baricadoes,
and the cleere stories toward the South north, are as lustrous as
Ebony: and yet complainest thou of obstruction?   35

MALVOLIO.   I am not mad sir *Topas*, I say to you this house is
darke.

CLOWN.   Madman thou errest: I say there is no darknesse but
ignorance, in which thou art more puzel'd then the Ægyptians
in their fogge.   40

MALVOLIO.   I say this house is as darke as Ignorance, thogh
Ignorance were as darke as hell; and I say there was never man
thus abus'd, I am no more madde then you are, make the triall
of it in any constant question.

CLOWN.   What is the opinion of *Pythagoras* concerning Wilde-   45
fowle?

MALVOLIO.   That the soule of our grandam, might happily
inhabite a bird.

CLOWN.   What thinkst thou of his opinion?

MALVOLIO.   I thinke nobly of the soule, and no way aprove his   50
opinion.

CLOWN.   Fare thee well: remaine thou still in darkenesse, thou
shalt hold th'opinion of *Pythagoras*, ere I will allow of thy wits,
and feare to kill a Woodcocke, lest thou dispossesse the soule of
thy grandam. Fare thee well.   55

MALVOLIO.   Sir *Topas*, sir *Topas*.

SIR TOBY.   My most exquisite sir *Topas*.

CLOWN.   Nay I am for all waters.

MARIA.   Thou mightst have done this without thy berd and
gowne, he sees thee not.   60

SIR TOBY.   To him in thine owne voyce, and bring me word
how thou findst him: I would we were well ridde of this knavery.
If he may bee conveniently deliver'd, I would he were, for I am
now so farre in offence with my Niece, that I cannot pursue with
any safety this sport to the uppeshot. Come by and by to my   65
Chamber.

Exit ⟨SIR TOBY *and* MARIA.⟩

IV. II. 34 stories] BLAKEWAY (*i.e.*, clere-stories); stores F; stones F2, 3, 4.

CLOWN. ⟨*Sings.*⟩ Hey Robin, jolly Robin, tell me how thy Lady does.

MALVOLIO. Foole.

CLOWN. My Lady is unkind, *perdie.*   70

MALVOLIO. Foole.

CLOWN. Alas why is she so?

MALVOLIO. Foole, I say.

CLOWN. She loves another. Who calles, ha?

MALVOLIO. Good foole, as ever thou wilt deserve well at my   75
hand, helpe me to a Candle, and pen, inke, and paper: as I am a
Gentleman, I will live to bee thankefull to thee for't.

CLOWN. M. *Malvolio?*

MALVOLIO. I good Foole.

CLOWN. Alas sir, how fell you besides your five witts?   80

MALVOLIO. Foole, there was never man so notoriouslie abus'd:
I am as well in my wits (foole) as thou art.

CLOWN. But as well: then you are mad indeede, if you be no
better in your wits then a foole.

MALVOLIO. They have heere propertied me: keepe mee in   85
darkenesse, send Ministers to me, Asses, and doe all they can to
face me out of my wits.

CLOWN. Advise you what you say: the Minister is heere. ⟨*In
feigned voice*⟩ Malvolio, Malvolio, thy wittes the heavens restore:
endeavour thy selfe to sleepe, and leave thy vaine bibble babble.   90

MALVOLIO. Sir *Topas.*

CLOWN. Maintaine no words with him good fellow. ⟨*In his own
voice*⟩ Who I sir, not I sir. God buy you good sir Topas: Marry
Amen. I will sir, I will.

MALVOLIO. Foole, foole, foole I say.   95

CLOWN. Alas sir be patient. What say you sir, I am shent for
speaking to you.

MALVOLIO. Good foole, helpe me to some light, and some
paper, I tell thee I am as well in my wittes, as any man in Illyria.

CLOWN. Well-a-day, that you were sir.   100

MALVOLIO. By this hand I am: good foole, some inke, paper,
and light: and convey what I will set downe to my Lady: it shall
advantage thee more, then ever the bearing of Letter did.

IV. II. 93–4 Marry Amen] *Some regard this as spoken in the Sir Topas voice; but
the colon suggests otherwise.*

CLOWN.   I will help you too't. But tel me true, are you not mad
 indeed, or do you but counterfeit?   105

MALVOLIO.   Beleeve me I am not, I tell thee true.

CLOWN.   Nay, Ile nere beleeve a madman till I see his brains.
 I will fetch you light, and paper, and inke.

MALVOLIO.   Foole, Ile requite it in the highest degree: I prethee be gone.   110

CLOWN.   ⟨*Sings*⟩ I am gone sir, and anon sir,
  Ile be with you againe:
 In a trice, like to the old vice,
  your neede to sustaine.
Who with dagger of lath, in his rage and his wrath,   115
  cries ah ha, to the divell:
Like a mad lad, paire thy nayles dad,
  Adieu good man divell.

                  Exit.

⟨SCENE III⟩

Enter SEBASTIAN.

SEBASTIAN.   This is the ayre, that is the glorious Sunne,
 This pearle she gave me, I do feel't, and see't,
 And though tis wonder that enwraps me thus,
 Yet 'tis not madnesse. Where's *Anthonio* then?
 I could not finde him at the Elephant,   5
 Yet there he was, and there I found this credite,
 That he did range the towne to seeke me out.
 His councell now might do me golden service,
 For though my soule disputes well with my sence,
 That this may be some error, but no madnesse,   10
 Yet doth this accident and flood of Fortune,
 So farre exceed all instance, all discourse,
 That I am readie to distrust mine eyes,
 And wrangle with my reason that perswades me
 To any other trust, but that I am mad,   15
 Or else the Ladies mad; yet if 'twere so,
 She could not sway her house, command her followers,
 Take, and give backe affayres, and their dispatch,

With such a smooth, discreet, and stable bearing
As I perceive she do's: there's something in't   20
That is deceiveable. But heere the Lady comes.

Enter OLIVIA, *and* PRIEST.

OLIVIA.   Blame not this haste of mine: if you meane well
    Now go with me, and with this holy man
    Into the Chantry by: there before him,
    And underneath that consecrated roofe,   25
    Plight me the full assurance of your faith,
    That my most jealious, and too doubtfull soule
    May live at peace. He shall conceale it,
    Whiles you are willing it shall come to note,
    What time we will our celebration keepe   30
    According to my birth, what do you say?
SEBASTIAN.   Ile follow this good man, and go with you,
    And having sworne truth, ever will be true.
OLIVIA.   Then lead the way good father, and heavens so shine,
    That they may fairely note this acte of mine.   35

                                                    Exeunt.

                Finis Actus Quartus.

                        ACT V

                      ⟨SCENE I⟩

                Enter CLOWN *and* FABIAN.

FABIAN.   Now as thou lov'st me, let me see his Letter.
CLOWN.   Good M. *Fabian*, grant me another request.
FABIAN.   Any thing.
CLOWN.   Do not desire to see this Letter.
FABIAN.   This is to give a dogge, and in recompence desire my   5
    dogge againe.

Enter DUKE, VIOLA, CURIO, *and* LORDS.
DUKE.   Belong you to the Lady *Olivia*, friends?
CLOWN.   I sir, we are some of her trappings.
DUKE.   I know thee well: how doest thou my good Fellow?

CLOWN.　Truely sir, the better for my foes, and the worse for my　10
friends.

DUKE.　Just the contrary: the better for thy friends.

CLOWN.　No sir, the worse.

DUKE.　How can that be?

CLOWN.　Marry sir, they praise me, and make an asse of me, now　15
my foes tell me plainly, I am an Asse: so that by my foes sir, I
profit in the knowledge of my selfe, and by my friends I am
abused: so that conclusions to be as kisses, if your foure negatives
make your two affirmatives, why then the worse for my friends,
and the better for my foes.　20

DUKE.　Why this is excellent.

CLOWN.　By my troth sir, no: though it please you to be one of
my friends.

DUKE.　Thou shalt not be the worse for me, there's gold.

CLOWN.　But that it would be double dealing sir, I would you　25
could make it another.

DUKE.　O you give me ill counsell.

CLOWN.　Put your grace in your pocket sir, for this once, and let
your flesh and blood obey it.

DUKE.　Well, I will be so much a sinner to be a double dealer:　30
there's another.

CLOWN.　*Primo, secundo, tertio*, is a good play, and the olde saying
is, the third payes for all: the triplex sir, is a good tripping
measure, or the belles of S. *Bennet* sir, may put you in minde, one,
two, three.　35

DUKE.　You can foole no more money out of mee at this throw:
if you will let your Lady know I am here to speak with her, and
bring her along with you, it may awake my bounty further.

CLOWN.　Marry sir, lullaby to your bountie till I come agen. I go
sir, but I would not have you to thinke, that my desire of having　40
is the sinne of covetousnesse: but as you say sir, let your bounty
take a nappe, I will awake it anon.

Exit.

Enter ANTONIO *and* OFFICERS.

VIOLA.　Here comes the man sir, that did rescue mee.

DUKE.　That face of his I do remember well,
Yet when I saw it last, it was besmear'd　45

As blacke as Vulcan, in the smoake of warre:
A bawbling Vessell was he Captaine of,
For shallow draught and bulke unprizable,
With which such scathfull grapple did he make,
With the most noble bottome of our Fleete,
That very envy, and the tongue of losse
Cride fame and honor on him: What's the matter?

FIRST OFFICER. Orsino, this is that *Anthonio*
That tooke the *Phœnix*, and her fraught from *Candy*,
And this is he that did the *Tiger* boord,
When your yong Nephew *Titus* lost his legge;
Heere in the streets, desperate of shame and state,
In private brabble did we apprehend him.

VIOLA. He did me kindnesse sir, drew on my side,
But in conclusion put strange speech upon me,
I know not what 'twas, but distraction.

DUKE. Notable Pyrate, thou salt-water Theefe,
What foolish boldnesse brought thee to their mercies,
Whom thou in termes so bloudie, and so deere
Hast made thine enemies?

ANTONIO. *Orsino*: Noble sir,
Be pleas'd that I shake off these names you give mee:
Anthonio never yet was Theefe, or Pyrate,
Though I confesse, on base and ground enough
Orsino's enemie. A witchcraft drew me hither:
That most ingratefull boy there by your side,
From the rude seas enrag'd and foamy mouth
Did I redeeme: a wracke past hope he was:
His life I gave him, and did thereto adde
My love without retention, or restraint,
All his in dedication. For his sake,
Did I expose my selfe (pure for his love)
Into the danger of this adverse Towne,
Drew to defend him, when he was beset:
Where being apprehended, his false cunning
(Not meaning to partake with me in danger)
Taught him to face me out of his acquaintance,
And grew a twentie yeeres removed thing
While one would winke: denide me mine owne purse,

50

55

60

65

70

75

80

Which I had recommended to his use,　　　　　85
Not halfe an houre before.

VIOLA.　How can this be?

DUKE.　When came he to this Towne?

ANTONIO.　To day my Lord: and for three months before,
No *intrim*, not a minutes vacancie,　　　　　90
Both day and night did we keepe companie.

Enter OLIVIA *and attendants.*

DUKE.　Heere comes the Countesse, now heaven walkes on earth:
But for thee fellow, fellow thy words are madnesse,
Three monthes this youth hath tended upon mee,
But more of that anon. Take him aside.　　　　　95

OLIVIA.　What would my Lord, but that he may not have,
Wherein *Olivia* may seeme serviceable?
Cesario, you do not keepe promise with me.

VIOLA.　Madam.

DUKE.　Gracious *Olivia*.　　　　　100

OLIVIA.　What do you say *Cesario*? Good my Lord.

VIOLA.　My Lord would speake, my dutie hushes me.

OLIVIA.　If it be ought to the old tune my Lord,
It is as fat and fulsome to mine eare
As howling after Musicke.　　　　　105

DUKE.　Still so cruell?

OLIVIA.　Still so constant Lord.

DUKE.　What to perversenesse? you uncivill Ladie
To whose ingrate, and unauspicious Altars
My soule the faithfull'st offrings have breath'd out　　　　　110
That ere devotion tender'd. What shall I do?

OLIVIA.　Even what it please my Lord, that shal becom him.

DUKE.　Why should I not, (had I the heart to do it)
Like to th'Egyptian theefe, at point of death
Kill what I love: (a savage jealousie,　　　　　115
That sometime savours nobly) but heare me this:
Since you to non-regardance cast my faith,
And that I partly know the instrument
That screwes me from my true place in your favour:
Live you the Marble-brested Tirant still.　　　　　120

But this your Minion, whom I know you love,
And whom, by heaven I sweare, I tender deerely,
Him will I teare out of that cruell eye,
Where he sits crowned in his masters spight.
Come boy with me, my thoughts are ripe in mischiefe: 125
Ile sacrifice the Lambe that I do love,
To spight a Ravens heart within a Dove.

VIOLA. And I most jocund, apt, and willinglie,
To do you rest, a thousand deaths would dye.

OLIVIA. Where goes *Cesario*? 130

VIOLA. After him I love,
More then I love these eyes, more then my life,
More by all mores, then ere I shall love wife.
If I do feigne, you witnesses above
Punish my life, for tainting of my love. 135

OLIVIA. Aye me detested, how am I beguil'd?

VIOLA. Who does beguile you? who does do you wrong?

OLIVIA. Hast thou forgot thy selfe? Is it so long?
Call forth the holy Father.

DUKE. Come, away. 140

OLIVIA. Whether my Lord? *Cesario*, Husband, stay.

DUKE. Husband?

OLIVIA. I Husband. Can he that deny?

DUKE. Her husband, sirrah?

VIOLA. No my Lord, not I. 145

OLIVIA. Alas, it is the basenesse of thy feare,
That makes thee strangle thy propriety:
Feare not *Cesario*, take thy fortunes up,
Be that thou know'st thou art, and then thou art
As great as that thou fear'st. 150

Enter PRIEST.

O welcome Father:
Father, I charge thee by thy reverence
Heere to unfold, though lately we intended
To keepe in darkenesse, what occasion now
Reveales before 'tis ripe: what thou dost know 155
Hath newly past, betweene this youth, and me.

PRIEST. A Contract of eternall bond of love,

Confirm'd by mutuall joynder of your hands,
Attested by the holy close of lippes,
Strengthned by enterchangement of your rings,   160
And all the Ceremonie of this compact
Seal'd in my function, by my testimony:
Since when, my watch hath told me, toward my grave
I have travail'd but two houres.

DUKE.   O thou dissembling Cub: what wilt thou be   165
When time hath sow'd a grizzle on thy case?
Or will not else thy craft so quickely grow,
That thine owne trip shall be thine overthrow?
Farewell, and take her, but direct thy feete,
Where thou, and I (henceforth) may never meet.   170

VIOLA.   My Lord, I do protest—

OLIVIA.   O do not sweare,
Hold little faith, though thou hast too much feare.

Enter SIR ANDREW.

SIR ANDREW.   For the love of God a Surgeon, send one presently to sir *Toby*.   175

OLIVIA.   What's the matter?

SIR ANDREW.   H'as broke my head a-crosse, and has given Sir
Toby a bloody Coxcombe too: for the love of God your helpe,
I had rather then forty pound I were at home.

OLIVIA.   Who has done this sir *Andrew*?   180

SIR ANDREW.   The Counts Gentleman, one *Cesario*: we tooke
him for a Coward, but hee's the verie divell incardinate.

DUKE.   My Gentleman *Cesario*?

SIR ANDREW.   Odd's lifelings heere he is: you broke my head
for nothing, and that that I did, I was set on to do't by sir *Toby*.   185

VIOLA.   Why do you speake to me, I never hurt you:
You drew your sword upon me without cause,
But I bespake you faire, and hurt you not.

Enter SIR TOBY *and* CLOWN.

SIR ANDREW.   If a bloody coxcombe be a hurt, you have hurt
me: I thinke you set nothing by a bloody Coxecombe. Heere   190
comes sir *Toby* halting, you shall heare more: but if he had not
beene in drinke, hee would have tickel'd you other gates then he
did.

DUKE.   How now Gentleman? how ist with you?

SIR TOBY.   That's all one, has hurt me, and there's th'end on't: 195
Sot, didst see Dicke Surgeon, sot?

CLOWN.   O he's drunke sir *Toby* an houre agone: his eyes were
set at eight i'th morning.

SIR TOBY.   Then he's a Rogue, and a passy measures pavyn: I
hate a drunken rogue.   200

OLIVIA.   Away with him? Who hath made this havocke with
them?

SIR ANDREW.   Ile helpe you sir *Toby*, because we'll be drest
together.

SIR TOBY.   Will you helpe, an Asse-head, and a coxcombe, and 205
a knave: a thin fac'd knave, a gull?

OLIVIA.   Get him to bed, and let his hurt be look'd too.

⟨*Exeunt* CLOWN, FABIAN, SIR TOBY *and* SIR ANDREW.⟩

Enter SEBASTIAN.

SEBASTIAN.   I am sorry Madam I have hurt your kinsman:
But had it beene the brother of my blood,
I must have done no lesse with wit and safety.   210
You throw a strange regard upon me, and by that
I do perceive it hath offended you:
Pardon me (sweet one) even for the vowes
We made each other, but so late ago.

DUKE.   One face, one voice, one habit, and two persons,   215
A naturall Perspective, that is, and is not.

SEBASTIAN.   *Anthonio*: O my deere *Anthonio*,
How have the houres rack'd, and tortur'd me,
Since I have lost thee?

ANTONIO.   *Sebastian* are you?   220

SEBASTIAN.   Fear'st thou that *Anthonio*?

ANTONIO.   How have you made division of your selfe,
An apple cleft in two, is not more twin
Then these two creatures. Which is *Sebastian*?

OLIVIA.   Most wonderfull.   225

SEBASTIAN.   Do I stand there? I never had a brother:
Nor can there be that Deity in my nature
Of heere, and every where. I had a sister,

Whom the blinde waves and surges have devour'd:
Of charity, what kinne are you to me?   230
What Countreyman? What name? What Parentage?

VIOLA.   Of *Messaline*: *Sebastian* was my Father,
Such a *Sebastian* was my brother too:
So went he suited to his watery tombe:
If spirits can assume both forme and suite,   235
You come to fright us.

SEBASTIAN.   A spirit I am indeed,
But am in that dimension grossely clad,
Which from the wombe I did participate.
Were you a woman, as the rest goes even,   240
I should my teares let fall upon your cheeke,
And say, thrice welcome drowned *Viola*.

VIOLA.   My father had a moale upon his brow.

SEBASTIAN.   And so had mine.

VIOLA.   And dide that day when *Viola* from her birth   245
Had numbred thirteene yeares.

SEBASTIAN.   O that record is lively in my soule,
He finished indeed his mortall acte
That day that made my sister thirteene yeares.

VIOLA.   If nothing lets to make us happie both,   250
But this my masculine usurp'd attyre:
Do not embrace me, till each circumstance,
Of place, time, fortune, do co-here and jumpe
That I am *Viola*, which to confirme,
Ile bring you to a Captaine in this Towne,   255
Where lye my maiden weeds: by whose gentle helpe,
I was preserv'd to serve this Noble Count:
All the occurrence of my fortune since
Hath beene betweene this Lady, and this Lord.

SEBASTIAN.   So comes it Lady, you have beene mistooke: 260
But Nature to her bias drew in that.
You would have bin contracted to a Maid,
Nor are you therein (by my life) deceiv'd,
You are betroth'd both to a maid and man.

DUKE.   Be not amaz'd, right noble is his blood: 265
If this be so, as yet the glasse seemes true,
I shall have share in this most happy wracke.

Boy, thou hast saide to me a thousand times,
Thou never should'st love woman like to me.

VIOLA. And all those sayings, will I over sweare,   270
And all those swearings keepe as true in soule,
As doth that Orbed Continent, the fire,
That severs day from night.

DUKE. Give me thy hand,
And let me see thee in thy womans weedes.   275

VIOLA. The Captaine that did bring me first on shore
Hath my Maides garments: he upon some Action
Is now in durance, at *Malvolio's* suite,
A Gentleman, and follower of my Ladies.

OLIVIA. He shall inlarge him: fetch *Malvolio* hither,   280
And yet alas, now I remember me,
They say poore Gentleman, he's much distract.

Enter CLOWN *with a Letter, and* FABIAN.

A most extracting frensie of mine owne
From my remembrance, clearly banisht his.
How does he sirrah?   285

CLOWN. Truely Madam, he holds *Belzebub* at the staves end as
well as a man in his case may do: has heere writ a letter to you,
I should have given't you to day morning. But as a madmans
Epistles are no Gospels, so it skilles not much when they are
deliver'd.   290

OLIVIA. Open't, and read it.

CLOWN. Looke then to be well edified, when the Foole delivers
the Madman. ⟨*In a loud voice*⟩ *By the Lord Madam.*

OLIVIA. How now, art thou mad?

CLOWN. No Madam, I do but reade madnesse: and your Lady- 295
ship will have it as it ought to bee, you must allow *Vox.*

OLIVIA. Prethee reade i'thy right wits.

CLOWN. So I do Madona: but to reade his right wits, is to reade
thus: therefore, perpend my Princesse, and give eare.

OLIVIA. Read it you, sirrah.   300

FABIAN. [*Reads*] By the Lord Madam, you wrong me, and the
world shall know it: Though you have put mee into darkenesse,
and given your drunken Cosine rule over me, yet have I the bene-
fit of my senses as well as your Ladieship. I have your owne letter,

that induced mee to the semblance I put on; with the which I 305
doubt not, but to do my selfe much right, or you much shame:
thinke of me as you please. I leave my duty a little unthought of,
and speake out of my injury. *The madly us'd Malvolio.*

OLIVIA.   Did he write this?

CLOWN.   I Madame.   310

DUKE.   This savours not much of distraction.

OLIVIA.   See him deliver'd *Fabian*, bring him hither:

⟨*Exit* FABIAN.⟩

My Lord, so please you, these things further thought on,
To thinke me as well a sister, as a wife,
One day shall crowne th'alliance on't, so please you,   315
Heere at my house, and at my proper cost.

DUKE.   Madam, I am most apt t'embrace your offer:
⟨*To* VIOLA⟩ Your Master quits you: and for your service done him,
So much against the mettle of your sex,
So farre beneath your soft and tender breeding,   320
And since you call'd me Master, for so long:
Heere is my hand, you shall from this time bee
Your Masters Mistris.

OLIVIA.   A sister, you are she.

Enter ⟨FABIAN *and*⟩ MALVOLIO.

DUKE.   Is this the Madman?   325

OLIVIA.   I my Lord, this same: How now *Malvolio*?

MALVOLIO.   Madam, you have done me wrong,
Notorious wrong.

OLIVIA.   Have I *Malvolio*? No.

MALVOLIO.   Lady you have, pray you peruse that Letter.   330
You must not now denie it is your hand,
Write from it if you can, in hand, or phrase,
Or say, tis not your seale, not your invention:
You can say none of this. Well, grant it then,
And tell me in the modestie of honor,   335
Why you have given me such cleare lights of favour,
Bad me come smiling, and crosse-garter'd to you,
To put on yellow stockings, and to frowne
Upon sir *Toby*, and the lighter people:

And acting this in an obedient hope,   340
Why have you suffer'd me to be imprison'd,
Kept in a darke house, visited by the Priest,
And made the most notorious gecke and gull,
That ere invention plaid on? Tell me why?
OLIVIA.   Alas *Malvolio*, this is not my writing,   345
Though I confesse much like the Charracter:
But out of question, tis *Marias* hand.
And now I do bethinke me, it was shee
First told me thou wast mad; then cam'st in smiling,
And in such formes, which heere were presuppos'd   350
Upon thee in the Letter: prethee be content,
This practice hath most shrewdly past upon thee:
But when we know the grounds, and authors of it,
Thou shalt be both the Plaintiffe and the Judge
Of thine owne cause.   355
FABIAN.   Good Madam heare me speake,
And let no quarrell, nor no braule to come,
Taint the condition of this present houre,
Which I have wondred at. In hope it shall not,
Most freely I confesse my selfe, and *Toby*   360
Set this device against *Malvolio* heere,
Upon some stubborne and uncourteous parts
We had conceiv'd against him. *Maria* writ
The Letter, at sir *Tobyes* great importance,
In recompence whereof, he hath married her: 365
How with a sportfull malice it was follow'd,
May rather plucke on laughter then revenge,
If that the injuries be justly weigh'd,
That have on both sides past.
OLIVIA.   Alas poore Foole, how have they baffel'd thee?   370
CLOWN.   Why some are borne great, some atchieve greatnesse,
and some have greatnesse throwne upon them. I was one sir, in
this Enterlude, one sir *Topas* sir, but that's all one: By the Lord
Foole, I am not mad: but do you remember, Madam, why laugh
you at such a barren rascall, and you smile not he's gag'd: and   375
thus the whirlegigge of time, brings in his revenges.
MALVOLIO.   Ile be reveng'd on the whole packe of you?

⟨*Exit.*⟩

OLIVIA.　He hath bene most notoriously abus'd.
DUKE.　Pursue him, and entreate him to a peace:
　　He hath not told us of the Captaine yet,　　　　　　　　380
　　When that is knowne, and golden time convents,
　　A solemne Combination shall be made
　　Of our deere soules. Meane time sweet sister,
　　We will not part from hence. *Cesario* come
　　(For so you shall be while you are a man:)　　　　　　　385
　　But when in other habites you are seene,
　　Orsino's Mistris, and his fancies Queene.
　　　　　　　　　　　　Exeunt ⟨*all but* CLOWN⟩.

CLOWN *sings*.
　　　　　When that I was and a little tine boy,
　　　　　　　with hey, ho, the winde and the raine:
　　　　　A foolish thing was but a toy,　　　　　　　390
　　　　　　　for the raine it raineth every day.

　　　　　But when I came to mans estate,
　　　　　　　with hey ho, etc.
　　　　　Gainst Knaves and Theeves men shut their gate,
　　　　　　　for the raine, etc.　　　　　　　395

　　　　　But when I came alas to wive,
　　　　　　　with hey ho, etc.
　　　　　By swaggering could I never thrive,
　　　　　　　for the raine, etc.

　　　　　But when I came unto my beds,　　　　　　　400
　　　　　　　with hey ho, etc.
　　　　　With tospottes still had drunken heades,
　　　　　　　for the raine, etc.

　　　　　A great while ago the world begon,
　　　　　　　with hey ho, etc.　　　　　　　405
　　　　　But that's all one, our Play is done,
　　　　　　　and wee'l strive to please you every day.
　　　　　　　　　　　　　　　⟨*Exit.*⟩

　　　　　　　　　　FINIS.

v. 1. 388 *tine*] F, *which never spells the word with a* "y"; *so also* F2, 3, 4; tiny
ROWE.

TEXTUAL NOTES

SIGLA

F = First Folio, 1623; F2, 3, 4 = second, third, fourth Folios.
om. = omits, is omitted by.
D.W. = *Twelfth Night*, ed. A. Quiller-Couch and J. Dover
Wilson. Cambridge, 1930.
SISSON = C. J. Sisson, *New Readings in Shakespeare*. Cambridge,
1956.
∼ = form of word(s) cited in lemma.
∧ = lack of punctuation.

Readings ascribed to older editors are from the Variorum Edn, ed.
H. H. Furness. Repr. New York, 1964.

I. I

ACT I / ⟨SCENE I⟩] *Actus
Primus, Scæna Prima.* F; *similarly throughout.*
10–11 capacitie ∧ . . . Sea, nought]
ROWE; ∼, . . . ∼. Nought F.
24 *Enter* VALENTINE] DYCE;
placed after ". . . her?" *in* F.

I. II

14 strong] F2; sttong F.
15 *Arion*] POPE; *Orion* F.
20 authoritie,] ROWE; ∼∧ F.

I. III

14 woer.] wooer. F2; ∼∧ F.
31 moreover] F2; moreour F.
35 Neece,] F2; ∼. F.
45 SIR ANDREW] *An.* F2; *Ma.* F.
Accost] ROWE; accost F.
acquaintance.] F2; ∼∧ F.

47 *Mary* Accost] ROWE; *Mary,*
accost F.
82 fencing,] F3; ∼∧ F.
88 me] F2; we F.
dos't] does't ROWE; dost F.
93 Count] F2; Connt F.
her.] F2; ∼, F.
94 Shee] She F2; *S*hee F.
95 swear't] CAPELL; swear t F;
sweare F2.
118 set] ROWE; sit F.
121 That's] F3; That F.

I. IV

6 favours?] F2; fauours. F.
7 VALENTINE. . . . me.] F *prints
as one line with* "he . . . fauours."
13 the] F2; rhe F.
22 returne.] F2; ∼, F.

I. V

15 absent;] MALONE; ∼, F.
20 points.] F2; ∼∧ F.

78   guiltlesse] F3; guitlesse F.

99   comes, one] MALONE; ~. One F.

100   *Enter* SIR TOBY.] *Placed after* "comes." *in* F.

146   *Enter* VIOLA.] F2; *Enter Violenta.* F.

148   will?] F4; ~. F.

158   I] F *prints only as catchword on* p. 258.

213   Inventoried,] F4; ~ₐ F.

225   him,] F3; ~ₐ F.

272   Messenger,] F3; ~ₐ F.

273   Counties] County's CAPELL; Countes F.
     him,] F2; ~ₐ F.

II. I

2   you?] F2; ~. F.

14   *Rodorigo*). My] ~)ₐ my F.

II. II

   doores.] F2;~, F (*apparently*).

4   sir):] ~)ₐ F.

17   That] F; ~ sure F2; ~ as DYCE.

28   our] F2; O F.

II. III

2   *Diluculo*] ROWE; *Deluculo* F.

7   life] ROWE; liues F.

11   drinke.] *The period is dropped below the line in* F; ~, F2.

19   In sooth] THEOBALD; Insooth F.

24   stocke.] *The period is imperceptible in some copies of* F.

98   go?] goe? F2; ~. F.

128   knight?] CAPELL; ~. F.

135   grounds] F; ground F2, *most editors.*

II. IV

1   Give ... frends.] F; JOHNSON *and* D.W. *make* "good ... frends" *parenthetical, to avoid the double* "Now"; *see* Note on Text.

9   it.] F2; ~? F.

14   love,] ROWE; ~ₐ F.

36   worne] F. HANMER'S "wonne", *though popular, is not necessary, unless* "worne" *was suggested by* "weares", l. 32.

81   world,] D.W.; ~ₐ F.

82–3   lands: ... her,] ~, ... ~: F.

87   sir?] POPE; ~. F.

88   I] HANMER; It F.

100   suffers] ROWE; suffer F.

105   know —] ROWE; ~. F.

II. V

5   rascally] D.W.; Rascally F.

67   plot.] ROWE; ~? F.

78   *C's*] F2; *C s* F.
     U's] F *uses a swash letter, which could mean* V *or* U; *V's* F2; *U's* F3; F4 *as* F.
     shee her] F2; shee het F.

86–7, 91–4   *Jove ... know. ... I ... life.*] F. *Arrangement and punctuation are obviously defective, but they may be intended as part of the fustian.*

88   alter'd] F2; alter d F.

112   sequell,] FURNESS; ~ₐ F.

123   borne] born ROWE, cp. III. IV. 39, V. I. 371; become F.
     atcheeve] F2, cp. *as above*; atcheeues F.

126   be,] ROWE; ~: F.

131   thee] F2; thce F.

133   fingers.] ROWE; ~ₐ F.

134   the] F2; tht F.

135   unhappy. Daylight] CAPELL; vnhappy ₐdaylight F.

136   politicke] F2; pollticke F.

145   garter'd] F2; Garter'd F.

149   *deere*] F2; *deero* F.

159   necke?] F2; ~. F.

III. I

   playing ... Tabor.] COLLIER.

7   King] F2; Kings F.

37   thee.] F2; *the period is raised in* F.

52 come;] ROWE; ∼, F.
63 wisemen folly-falne] wise men,
    folly-faln CAPELL; wisemens folly
    falne F.
67 ousie;] ∼ₐ F.
78 MARIA] ROWE; *Gentlewoman* F.
89 service.] F2; seruiceₐ F.
94 Y'are;] F3; y'are F.
96 Your] F3; your F.
108 here] THIRLBY; heare F; hear F3.
116–22 That ... enemies]. *Line-*
    arrangement as F; *variously*
    divided by editors.
130 Your] F2; your F.
134 You'll] F2; you'l F.
    me?] ROWE; ∼: F.
142–3 beautifull, ... lip?] ∼? ...
    ∼, F.

III. II

1 longer.] F3; ∼: F.
7 thee the] F3; the F.
    that?] F2; ∼. F.
10 me?] F2; ∼. F.
28 him,] F3; ∼ₐ F.
39 go,] CAPELL; ∼ₐ F.
69 Ladie] F; *some copies have a type-*
    mark like a comma.

III. III

8 travell] F2; rrauell F.
12 feare,] POPE; ∼ₐ F.
21 Lodging.] F2; ∼? F.
22 night,] F2; ∼ₐ F.
50 for] COLLIER; For F.

III. IV

7 but] POPE; But F.
13, 15 F *gives no exit for Maria, and*
    places Malvolio's entry after l.
    13.
15 merry] F3; metry F; mercy F2.
19 Sad,] THEOBALD; ∼ₐ F.
19, 20 this] THEOBALD; This F.
36 Lady?] F2; ∼. F.
51 let] F2; ler F.
57 look'd] F2; look d F.

65 tang] CAPELL, cp. II. v. 128;
    langer with F; tang with F2, 3, 4.
    "With" *is probably intrusive*
    from l. 64.
76 sanctity?] F2; ∼. F.
104 Sathan.] sathan F, *with a dubious*
    period; Satan. F4.
137 Law.] F3; ∼ₐ F.
143 me —] ROWE; ∼. F.
151 If ... cannot:] F *has the speech*
    heading "To." before this line.
152 You ... fit ... for't] F2; Yon
    ... sit ... fot't F.
156 it] F2; F *has* "t", *preceded by a*
    space.
177 on't] F. THEOBALD'S "out",
    though popular, is needless, since
    the suggestion is of a sacrifice.
187 give?] F4; ∼. F.
190 you?] F2; ∼. F.
196 thee] F2; the F.
219 competent] F4; computent F.
241 hee's] hee s F; he's F2.
287 FIRST OFFICER.] 1. *Off.* F, *and*
    similarly thereafter (also "2
    Off.").
288 *Orsino.*] F2; ∼ₐ F.
295–6 do, ... purse?] DYCE; ∼:
    ... ∼. F.
311 perswasion?] F2; ∼. F.
318 lying,] F; ∼ₐ ROWE, *and many*
    editors.
341 prove true] F2; proue ttue F.
357 sword.] F3; ∼ₐ F.
358 not —] not, — THEOBALD; ∼. F.

IV. I

8–9 I ... me.] CAPELL; F *prints as*
    prose.
13 Lady.] ∼? F.
15–17 I ... paiment.] CAPELL; F
    prints as prose.
59 me.] F2; ∼ₐ F.

IV. II

5 in such] F *has* "such" *as*
    catchword on p. 270, *and starts*

p.271 *with* "in such", "in" *being badly alined.*

29   Sathan] F2; sathan F.
37   darke.] F2; ∼, F (*apparently*).
65   to] ROWE; *om.* F.
105   counterfeit?] F2; ∼. F.
107   brains.] D.W.; ∼∧ F; braines, F2.

IV. III

1   SEBASTIAN.] *Seb.* F2; *om.* F.
4   then?] F2; ∼, F.
7   out.] ROWE; ∼, F.

V. I

45   Yet] F2; yet F.
99   Madam.] F2; ∼: F; ∼? CAPELL.
112   him.] F2; ∼∧ F.
168   overthrow?] F2; ouerthrow: F.
171   protest —] ROWE; ∼. F.

179   home] F2; homc F.
182   incardinate] F2; incardinatc F.
187   You] F2; you F.
199   pavyn] Pavin F2; panyn F.
205   helpe,] ∼∧ F.
267   wracke.] F2; ∼, F.
273   from] F2; ftom F.
285   sirrah] F; *the first* "r" *is faint, leading* FURNESS *and* D.W. *to record* F *as* "si rah".
323   Your] F2; your F.
363   against] F; *in* TYRWHITT, *as the idiom is awkward.*
372   throwne] F; thrust THEOBALD. cp. II. V. 124, III. IV. 43.
373   Lord] F2; Lotd F.
381   convents,] F2; ∼∧ F.
402   With] F; We POLLARD (D.W.).
405   with] F2; *om.* F.

COMMENTARY

D.W. = *Twelfth Night*, ed. A. Quiller-Couch and J. Dover Wilson,
Cambridge 1930.

I. I

3 appetite] Not "love", but "love's appetite for music". Love accepts anything that feeds it, then tires of it by surfeit (ll. 10–13). Orsino is a connoisseur of love, and does not wish it to end.

5 sound] The melody is as sweet as music heard across a bank of flowers, whose scent seems drawn along with it; emendation ("south", "sough") is not needed.

14–15 so . . . fantasticall] The lover's mind is so full of imagined figures that it alone reaches the full height of creative imagination.

22 Hart] As Actæon in Ovid was turned into a "hart" by the outraged virginity of Diana, and torn by her hounds, so his "heart" is torn by the passions roused by Olivia's purity.

27 heate] Either a noun = circuit of a course — "the end of a cycle of seven years" — or a participle = heated — "till seven years have been warmed by the sun". "Till" = "to the end of". D.W. reads "hence" (Rowe).

36 golden shaft] Cupid's golden arrow causes love, his leaden destroys it (Ovid).

38–40 When . . . king] "When the three ruling powers of her nature (liver = passion) are occupied (supply'd) like thrones, and when

her whole being (sweet perfections) is completed (fill'd) by her own beloved master. . . ." A comma after "supply'd" would help.

I. II

2 Illyria] On contemporary maps identified with "Sclavonia", stretching from the north-east coast of the Adriatic through Slovenia and Croatia. Reputedly a piratical land, and probably remembered from Plautus, *Menaechmi*, 235.

40–1 sight And company] Hanmer's "company And sight" mends the metre; but F supplies a natural climax, as "company" implies courtship.

44 made . . . mellow] "Brought to maturity my chosen time . . .".

58 Eunuch] Boy *castrati* were often employed as court singers. Nothing more is heard of the plan; either Shakespeare or Viola had second thoughts.

I. III

5 except . . . excepted] Toby uses a formula from leases ("apart from matters previously excepted") to mean "let her take exception as she has done before": but the sense slides drunkenly into a pun on "accept" also.

36 parish top] A large top kept in villages to exercise the peasants in winter: probably the remnant of an imitative ritual, since the world is sometimes shown emblematically as a top: cp. "whirlegigge", v. 1. 376.

37 *Castiliano vulgo*] Unexplained, perhaps corrupt. Usually taken as "Put on your solemn (Castilian) manners in public". But "Castile" is a drinking term; and Castilian/ Castalian were sometimes confused.

40 Shrew] Andrew mangles fashionable speech; does he mean "mouse"? cp. I. v. 54.

44 Chamber-maid] Toby's joke, the source of much critical error. Maria is a gentlewoman, cp. I. v. 143.

51 company] The audience.

60–7 Now . . . jest] Maria quotes the proverb (= "I think what I like"), then echoes Andrew's remark about having "fooles in hand" with the invitation traditional among servant girls when asking for a present in return for a kiss ("bring . . . drinke"). Andrew fails to understand, so the jest is "dry", as a dry hand denotes amorous timidity.

76 beefe] Elizabethan medicine held that excessive eating of beefe caused "gross blood" and melancholy.

82–4 tongues . . . haire] "Tongues" and "tongs" were pronounced alike. Flax (l. 89) hangs straight down.

103 old man] Probably = "old hand, expert". Theobald read "nobleman".

111 mistris *Mals* picture] Unexplained. Suggestions include Moll Frith, also called Moll Cutpurse (a contemporary "roaring girl"); Mary Fitton, mistress of Pembroke, and beloved of Knollys; and Maria herself. The dialogue at I. v. 200 suggests that "Mal" might

mean "Ol-ivia": but I can find no authority for this abbreviation.

121 Taurus] The zodiacal sign governing neck and throat; Andrew gets it wrong, and Toby complicates the jest.

<h3 style="text-align:center">I. IV</h3>

34 sound] "Unbroken". Emendation (*e.g.*, "in" or "of" for "and") is unnecessary.

<h3 style="text-align:center">I. V</h3>

4–27 well hang'de. . . . best] Linked badinage; see Glossary, *s.vv.* colours, lenton, points, gaskins, dishonest (l. 36). Feste says that he who is sexually strong ("well hang'de", supposed to be an endowment of fools) needs fear no excuses. Maria asks for a respectable (good, lenten) version of the joke, and gets it in terms of hanging ("collars") and the military sense of "colours". She retorts that he has been with the whores, not the wars (cp. "lemon", II. III. 22, and *Timon*, IV. III. 61). He turns his talents/talons (cp. *Love's Labour's Lost*, IV. II. 65) on her and her plan to marry Toby. She retorts that he has difficulty in keeping his breeches on, and had better be careful. This reading, based partly on Hotson, affects our view of Feste's character.

31 *Quinapalus*] Unidentified, like the rest of Feste's professional "Rabelaisian" erudition; perhaps = his bauble.

44 As . . . flower] Olivia is wedded to calamity by her mourning vow, but like all women she will be unfaithful since beauty is so transient.

48–9 *Cucullus . . . monachum*] Proverbial: "the cowl makes not the monk".

52 ff. Madona] "My lady"; Hotson suggests a pun, = Mad donna.

73 stone] Perhaps a glance at Stone, the professional fool. "Ordinary" means "eating-house", suggesting a place of vulgar entertainment.

97–8 as if . . . foole] *i.e.*, "wisely", from the proverb "A wise man commonly has a fool to his heir", cp. II. III. 40, where "wise mans sonne" = fool.

112 faith] To defy the "devil" at the gate.

161 phangs] "I challenge my worst enemy to deny . . ."

178 Giant] The boy playing Maria must have been very small.

198 method] Preaching style, as in "text" and "chapter".

204 such . . . present] Portraits were usually dated with the age of the subject, and the formula "*ætatis suæ . . .*". See Glossary, *s.v.* present.

218 divell] As the type of pride.

237 willow] As the symbol of rejected love.

II. I

14–15 *Rodorigo . . . Messaline*] The reason for the change of name is not made clear. Messaline, unknown to geography, may be a half-memory of "Massiliensis", Plautus, *Menaechmi*, 235.

II. II

6–7 desperate assurance] Certainty that his case is hopeless.

10 She . . . it] Viola's quick wit supplies this explanation.

II. III

2 *Diluculo surgere . . .*] ". . . saluberrimum est": "to rise at dawn is best for the health"; from Lily's Latin Grammar.

14–15 Picture . . . three] A sign showing two fools or asses, in-

scribed "we three", the spectator being the third.

20–1 *Pigrogromitus . . . Queubus*] Unexplained.

23–5 impeticos . . . houses] "Impeticot" = "impetticoat" (Johnson) may well be the right reading. "I pocketed (or better, "spent on my petticoat or wench") your miserable gratuity; for M. may suspect but cannot punish me. My girl is high-class, and the Myrmidons not a low pub". The interpretation is doubtful. The passage suggests that Feste's costume is the long child's "petticoat" sometimes worn by fools (Hotson).

35 *O Mistris mine . . .*] A tune so entitled is in Morley's *Consort Lessons* (1599), and was arranged by Byrd for virginals (1603). Probably there is no direct connexion with the play, all versions being variants on some popular song.

50–2 contagious . . . contagion] Andrew's erudite "mellifluous voice" amuses Toby, who plays on the two senses of "contagious" ("catchy" and "catching", *i.e.*, malodorous, as of the plague), and produces the matching phrase "a contagious breath". Andrew fails to see the joke, so Toby retorts, in effect, "You are calling it a sweet-sounding stink, which is like mixing up your nose and year ears". "Contagious" is found in Riche, of "passions".

55 Weaver] Since many weavers were Calvinist refugees from the Netherlands, they were traditionally supposed to be fond of psalm-singing.

59 *Thou Knave*] Extant in a collection of 1609; each singer calls the other a knave.

70 Peg-a-ramsie] Unexplained, except as the title of a rude song and a
dance. I suspect Toby is deliberate-
ly mangling Andrew's muddled
"Pigrogromitus". See Glossary, *s.v.*
Catayan.

70 *Three merry men*] A quatrain
first found in Peele's *Old Wives'
Tale*, *c.*1592.

71 tilly vally. Ladie] Often punctu-
ated "tilly vally, Ladie!", continu-
ing Toby's scorn for the threat of
"my Lady". The song is the ballad
of the constant Susanna, found
*c.*1562, and echoed in *Romeo and
Juliet*, II. IV.

76 *O the twelfe ...*] From the old
ballad of "Musselburgh Field"
(Kittredge, 1966).

91 Farewell deere heart ...] The
opening of "Corydon's Farewell
to Phyllis", found in Jones's *First
Booke of Ayres*, 1600. Jones says he
has published the "private efforts"
of "divers gentlemen without their
consents".

104–5 Cakes ... Ginger] Spiced
cakes and ale were served for holi-
days and saints' days, and disliked
by Puritans (cp. Jonson, *Bartholo-
mew Fair*, I. I.). St Anne finds
husbands for girls. Ginger was supposed an aphrodisiac, as well as a
spice.

107 Chaine] Sign of the steward's
office: = "Get on with your job as
a steward."

112 shake your eares] "when men
doe mocke any body, thei wagge
their handes up and doun by their
eares at the sides of their hed and
doe counterfeact the facion of an
Asses eares ... the Asse also
appereth by waggying his eares vp
and doun to mocke & skorne
folkes ...": Udall (1542), quoted
by Hulme, H. M., *Explorations in

Shakespeare's Language*, 1962, p.
198.

118 patient for to night] By an early
Church custom, in memory of the
story of Tobias, or Toby, the
groom was expected to abstain the
first night: a knowing *double-
entendre.*

156–8 *Penthisilea ... beagle*] Two
more jokes on Maria's size: the
beagle has short legs, and Penthisilea, Queen of the Amazons,
was no doubt large.

II. IV

1–2 Now ... Now] See pp. 11 and 86.

55 *Come away ...*] Not elsewhere
found; it is not "old and plain",
but a polished lute-song, apt to the
Duke's mood.

74 changeable] Orsino's inconstancy
is like the colours of taffeta or opal,
or the shifting sea. "Makes ...
nothing" = "renders a profitable
voyage null", but the ambiguous
phrasing makes it sound like a
compliment.

117–18 Patience ... greefe] A statue
of Patience bearing her grief with a
smile of resignation. See Glossary,
s.v. green.

120 Our ... will] Our outward signs
of love are greater than our real
passion.

II. V

34 *Strachy. ... wardrobe*] Countless
conjectures, none convincing. Sisson discovered a William Strachey,
d. 1621, a sharer in the Blackfriars,
and a Yeomans who was its ward-
robe-master. If some theatrical
scandal is meant, this is an actor's
gag, and late: but there is no sign of
textual disturbance.

57 cars] Torn asunder by chariots;
from Plautus, *Menaechmi*, 862 ff.

80 why that?] "Any sailor could explain the joke" (Harrison); but broad bawdy is out of place here. Perhaps the actors have been tampering.

83 *Lucrece*] Sealed with an impression of the head (probably) of Lucrece, type of chastity.

93 *M.O.A.I.*] Unexplained; perhaps meant for "I AM O(livia)" (Cox).

107-8 Sowter ... Fox] Sowter (= cobbler), a hound's name. Probably means that Malvolio is like a stupid hound, which, when hunting a hare, gives tongue at the scent of a fox.

130-1 yellow ... crosse garter'd] Yellow, the colour of Spain and jealousy; cross-gartering, fashionable in the 1560s, now outmoded and Puritanical.

152 Sophy] Shah of Persia; see p. 1.

III. I

2 Tabor] The contemporary picture of Tarlton shows him playing tabor and pipe, and dancing; probably Feste performed between acts.

19 bonds ... them] See p. 11; if there is a particular reference, it is unclear. Some read "bawds".

51 *Cressida* was a begger] In Henryson's *Testament of Cresseid* (included in sixteenth-century editions of Chaucer) she becomes a leprous beggar. Shakespeare's *Troilus and Cressida* is dated c.1601.

132 Westward hoe] Cry of Thames watermen, going from the city to Westminster; perhaps = "Then I return to Orsino's court". Hotson uses this passage in placing his stage "houses" according to the points of the compass; Olivia's is east, and Orsino's west.

150-3 Do ... better] "Do not advance the forced argument that because I offer love unsought, you should not return it; rather link one argument to another, to conclude that though it is good to seek love, to gain it unsought is better".

III. II

20 double gilt] Gilt plate was made by washing twice with gold.

23 Dutchmans beard] Probably Barentz, whose voyage of 1596/7 was described in a book of 1598. A detail from it appears on Wright's map, cp. l. 67.

36 thou'st] "Thou" is informal, ruder than "you".

39 bedde of *Ware*] This great bed, nearly 11 ft. wide, is now in the Victoria and Albert Museum.

43 Cubiculo] Probably = "private chamber". D.W. reads "thy cubicle".

56 youngest ... mine] "Wren" and "youngest" for Maria's size. "Mine" because she is his girl. There is no need to emend to "nine" because wrens lay a lot of eggs.

64-5 Pedant ... Church] To use the church as a school-room was old-fashioned.

67 new Mappe] See p. 1. Wright's was the first English map of the world to use the projection now called Mercator's. The many rhumb-lines suggest wrinkles. "Augmentation" does not mean "addition", or "increase in size" (D.W.), as comparison with other maps shows; it probably means "more detailed representation"— or possibly "heraldic decoration", with reference to the large coat of arms covering north-west America. The map is reproduced in the 1903

edition of Hakluyt. The identi-
fication is not beyond question.

III. III

42 Elephant] Presumably the South
London inn, the Elephant and
Castle.

III. IV

34 Nightingales ... Dawes] "To
answer you is like a nightingale
talking to a jackdaw".

92 Carry... woman] "Wise women"
like Mother Bombie dealt in popular
remedies as well as fortunes;
analysis of urine was standard
medical practice.

104 Colliar] Colliers (sellers, or
miners, of coal) are black and work
underground, so typifying Satan.

210 carpet consideration] A "carpet
knight" is one dubbed on a peaceful
not a warlike occasion.

242 firago] "Virago" always implies
a woman; Toby glances at Cesario's
timidity, while frightening Andrew
with a "learned" word suggesting
fire.

286 Hee] *i.e.*, the horse.

334 trunkes] Taken as clothes-chests,
elaborately decorated with carving
or painting: an odd metaphor.
Perhaps dead trees, overgrown with
parasitical foliage?

IV. I

8 Vent] "Utter": common enough.
Feste perhaps finds it funny because of its anatomical sense (cp.
cockney), or because of the pun on
"vent" = "sell". His money sense
is well developed.

20 purchase] To buy a property for a
sum equivalent to 14 years' rent
would be unusually expensive; so
the meaning is that they pay high
for a good reputation.

54 started] "Start" = to drive a
beast (heart/hart) from cover.

IV. II

2 sir *Topas*] "Sir" was a courtesy
title of priests (curate = vicar).
Topas because the topaz was held
to cure lunacy; and cp. the pedant
Sir Tophas in Lyly's *Endimion*.

11-13 *Prage ... Gorbodacke*] More
baffling erudition. The story of
Gorboduc was familiar, not only
from the tragedy of that name
(1562), but from *The Faerie Queene*
(II. X. 34), and Geoffrey of Mon-
mouth's *History*, where it is close
to the story of Lear. If Illyria =
"Sclavonia", Prague may be vaguely
supposed to be within its bound-
aries. *Parismus* also has a hermit.

31 house] A small enclosed room
(dark, as proper for madmen), like
the theatrical "house" or "mansion"
cp. III. I. 132. Feste pretends to
describe a "house" in the larger
sense; Hotson and Akrigg find
points of resemblance to Whitehall
and the Middle Temple respectively.

40 fogge] The ninth Egyptian plague,
Exodus, X. 21-3.

45 *Pythagoras*] His doctrine of trans-
migration of souls was common
knowledge, *e.g.*, from Ovid's *Meta-
morphoses*.

67 Hey Robin...] An early sixteenth-
century ballad reprinted in Percy's
Reliques.

113 old vice] This comic figure of the
old interludes sometimes wore a
fool's long coat and wooden
dagger, and fought the devil
(= Malvolio), whose nails he tried
to cut.

IV. III

26 Plight] The ceremony is one of
betrothal, not marriage, but legally
binding.

V. I

5 dogge] Manningham's diary for 26 Mar. 1603 tells precisely such a story of Elizabeth and her kinsman Dr Bullein.

18–19 conclusions ... affirmatives] "To stop the argument as with a kiss, since in kissing, as in grammar, a lady's 'No, no' means 'yes', I can make the two following affirmative statements. ..." So editors; but some stage-business seems to be required.

32 *Primo* ...] A children's game.

34 S. *Bennet*] Stow mentions four London churches of St Bennet (Benedict); one was near the Globe. Nothing is known of the bells.

51 tongue of losse] Voices of those who lost the battle.

54 *Candy*] Candia, Crete.

54–5 *Phoenix ... Tiger*] Oddly, both are inn-names in the *Comedy of Errors*; the *Tiger* was a famous ship, whose name reappears in *Macbeth*.

89 Three months] Shakespearian "double time"; in "fact", the action of the play covers three days.

114 Egyptian theefe] In Heliodorus' *Ethiopica* (English version 1569) the bandit Thyamis tries to kill his beloved Chariclea, but kills another by mistake.

177 H'as broke] This must be a second quarrel, not accounted for in the play; in the theatre, nobody notices.

182 incardinate] Andrew's version of "incarnate".

184 Odd's lifelings] "God's little life": a minimal oath.

199 passy measures pavyn] "Passamezzo pavane": the surgeon is a slow-paced humbug. The music for a pavane was "set at eight" bars, hence the association.

216 naturall Perspective] Nature acts like a "perspective", an optical glass designed to present an illusion: but as the word also means "telescope", there is a suggestion that truth and illusion are one—a point developed further at l. 266.

261 bias] Natural inclination, a metaphor from bowls.

266 glasse] The perspective glass of l. 216 now shows true.

272 Orbed Continent] "Spherical container": *i.e.*, the Ptolemaic sphere which holds the sun ("the fire ... night").

278 durance] We have heard nothing of this: a device to bring Malvolio back on stage.

289 Epistles ... Gospels] Punning on the Biblical senses, and perhaps suggesting that the Epistles have less authority than the Gospels.

363–5 *Maria ... married her*] A gentlemanly but not quite true account of what happened.

388 ff. *When that I was ...*] In *Lear*, III. II. 74, the fool (Armin) sings another stanza of this. Dover Wilson regards the *Lear* quatrain as Shakespeare's, and the present song as Armin's adaptation. Early editors found it merely clownish; today, most see it as summing up the theme of the play.

390 *foolish thing*] His bauble (perhaps with sexual undertones) as a sign of human folly.

BIBLIOGRAPHY

ABBREVIATIONS

P.M.L.A. = *Publications of the Modern Language Association of America*
S.Q. = *Shakespeare Quarterly*
S.S. = *Shakespeare Survey*

I. SHAKESPEARE'S WORK IN GENERAL

A. TEXTUAL

Texts and Editions

Comedies, Histories, and Tragedies. *First Folio, 1623; second Folio, 1632; third Folio, 1664; fourth Folio, 1685.

Comedies, Histories, and Tragedies. Facsimile of First Folio, ed. S. Lee, Oxford 1902.

Comedies, Histories, and Tragedies. Facsimile of First Folio, ed. H. Kökeritz, London 1955.

Works, ed. J. Munro. London 1958.

Books and Articles

GREG, W. W. *The Shakespeare First Folio.* Oxford 1955.

HINMAN, C. *The Printing and Proof-Reading of the First Folio of Shakespeare.* Oxford 1963.

SISSON, C. J. *New Readings in Shakespeare.* Cambridge 1956.

B. CRITICAL

A Companion to Shakespeare Studies, edd. H. GRANVILLE-BARKER and G. B. HARRISON. Cambridge 1934.

ALEXANDER, P. *Shakespeare's Life and Art.* London 1939.

BARBER, C. L. *Shakespeare's Festive Comedy.* Princeton, N.J. 1959.

BETHELL, S. L. *Shakespeare and the Popular Dramatic Tradition.* London 1948.

BRADBROOK, M. C. *Shakespeare and Elizabethan Poetry.* London 1951.

BROWN, J. R. *Shakespeare and his Comedies.* London 1957.

BULLOUGH, G. See *Narrative and Dramatic Sources of Shakespeare*.

CHAMBERS, E. K. *William Shakespeare*. Oxford 1930.

CHARLTON, H. B. *Shakespearian Comedy*. London 1938.

CECIL, D. *The Fine Art of Reading*. London 1957.

COGHILL, N. "The Basis of Shakespearian Comedy", in *Essays and Studies*, n.s., III (1950), pp. 1–28.

———. *Shakespeare's Professional Skills*. Cambridge 1964.

CRANE, M. "Shakespeare's Comedies and the Critics", in *S.Q.*, XV (1964), p. 67–73.

DOREN, M. VAN. *Shakespeare*. New York; repr. Anchor Books n.d.

EVANS, B. *Shakespeare's Comedies*. Oxford 1960.

GOLDSMITH, R. H. *Wise Fools in Shakespeare*. Liverpool 1958.

GORDON, G. *Shakespearian Comedy*. Oxford 1945.

GRANVILLE-BARKER, H. See *A Companion to Shakespeare Studies*.

GRIVELET, M. "Shakespeare as 'Corrupter of Words'", in *S.S.*, XVI (1963), pp. 70–5.

HARRISON, G. B. *Shakespeare at Work: 1692–1603*. Ann Arbor 1958.

———. See *A Companion to Shakespeare Studies*.

HARTNOLL, P. See *Shakespeare in Music*.

HOTSON, L. *Shakespeare's Motley*. London 1952.

HUNTER, G. K. "The Later Comedies", in *Shakespeare the Writer and his Work*, ed. B. Dobrée, London 1964, pp. 181–238.

KERMODE, F. "The Mature Comedies", in *Stratford-upon-Avon Studies*, III (1961), pp. 211–227.

LONG, J. H. *Shakespeare's Use of Music*. Gainesville, Fla., 1955.

MAHOOD, M. M. "Love's Confined Doom", in *S.S.*, XV (1962), pp. 50–61.

MAXWELL, J. C. "The Middle Plays", in *The Age of Shakespeare*, ed. B. Ford, London 1955.

MUIR, K. *Shakespeare's Sources, I. Comedies and Tragedies*. London 1957.

Narrative and Dramatic Sources of Shakespeare, ed. G. BULLOUGH, London 1958.

NOSWORTHY, J. M. "Music and its Function in the Romances of Shakespeare", in *S.S.*, XI (1958), pp. 60–9.

ONIONS, C. T. *A Shakespeare Glossary*. Oxford 1949.

PARROTT, T. M. *Shakespearean Comedy*. New York 1949.

PETTET, E. C. *Shakespeare and the Romance Tradition*. London 1949.

Shakespeare in Music, ed. P. HARTNOLL, London 1964.

THOMPSON, K. F. "Shakespeare's Romantic Comedies", in *P.M.L.A.*, LXVII (1952), pp. 1079–93.

WAIN, J. *The Living World of Shakespeare*. London 1966.

WATKINS, R. *On Producing Shakespeare*. London 1950.

WELSFORD, E. *The Fool*. Gloucester, Mass., 1966 (original publication 1935).

WILSON, J. D. *Shakespeare's Happy Comedies*. London 1962.

II. *TWELFTH NIGHT*

A. TEXTUAL

Texts and Editions

Twelfth Night. A Facsimile of the First Folio Text, with an Introduction by J. Dover Wilson, London n.d.

Twelfth Night, ed. H. H. Furness, Variorum Edn, New York 1901; reprinted 1964.

Twelfth Night, edd. A. T. Quiller-Couch and J. Dover Wilson, New Cambridge Edn, Cambridge 1930.

Twelfth Night, ed. M. Luce, Arden Edn, revised, London 1937.

Twelfth Night, ed. G. B. Harrison, Penguin Edn, London 1937; reprinted 1964.

Twelfth Night, ed. C. T. Prouty, Pelican Edn, Baltimore 1958.

Twelfth Night, ed. A. C. Ward, London 1962.

Twelfth Night, edd. G. L. Kittredge and I. Ribner, Waltham, Mass.; 2nd edn, 1966.

Articles

YAMADA, A. "The Textual Problems of *Twelfth Night*, 1623", in *Bulletin of the Liberal Arts Department, Mie University* (Japan), XXVI (July 1962), pp. 57–63.

B. CRITICAL

AKRIGG, G. P. V., "*Twelfth Night* at the Middle Temple", in *S.Q.*, IX (1958), pp. 422–4.

BRADLEY, A. C. "Feste the Jester", in *A Miscellany*, London 1929, pp. 207–17; originally published 1916.

BRITTIN, N. A. "The *Twelfth Night* of Shakespeare and of Professor Draper" in *S.Q.*, VII (1956), pp. 211–16.

COX, L. S. "The Riddle in *Twelfth Night*", in *S.Q.*, XIII (1962), p. 360.

CRANE, M. "*Twelfth Night* and Shakespearian Comedy", in *S.Q.*, VI (1955), pp. 1–8.

DRAPER, J. W. *The Twelfth Night of Shakespeare's Audience*. Stanford and London 1950.

HOLLANDER, J. "*Twelfth Night* and the Morality of Indulgence", in *Sewanee Review*, LXVII (1959), pp. 220–38.

HOTSON, L. *The First Night of Twelfth Night*. London 1961.

KAUFMAN, H. A. "Nicolò Secchi as a Source of *Twelfth Night*", in *S.Q.*, V (1954), pp. 271–80.

LAMB, C. "On Some of the Old Actors", in *Essays of Elia*, London 1868, pp. 171–182.

MARKELS, J. "Shakespeare's Confluence of Tragedy and Comedy: *Twelfth Night* and *King Lear*", in *S.Q.*, XV (1964), pp. 75–88.

MARSH, N. "A Note on a Production of *Twelfth Night*", in *S.S.*, VIII (1955), pp. 69–73.

MUESCHKE, P., and J. FLEISHER. "Jonsonian Elements in the Comic Underplot of *Twelfth Night*", in *P.M.L.A.*, XLVIII (1933), pp. 722–40.

NAGARAJAN, S. " "What You Will": A Suggestion", in *S.Q.*, X (1959), pp. 61–7.

RACE, S. "Manningham's Diary. The Case for Re-examination", in *Notes and Queries*, CXCIX (1954), pp. 380–3.

SALINGAR, L. G. "The design of *Twelfth Night*", in *S.Q.*, IX (1958), pp. 117–39.

SISSON, C. J. "Tudor Intelligence Tests: Malvolio and Real Life", in *Essays on Shakespeare and Elizabethan Drama*, ed. R. Hosley, London 1963.

TAYLOR, M. A. "He that Did the Tiger Board", in *S.Q.*, XV (1964), pp. 110–13.

WILLIAMS, P. "Mistakes in *Twelfth Night* and their Resolution", in *P.M.L.A.*, LXXVI (1961), pp. 193–9.

GLOSSARY

Words are spelt as in the text. Normally only the first occurrence of a word or sense is noted.

abatement	*depreciation in value*, I. I. 13.
accost	*greet politely, a currently fashionable term*, I. III. 42.
admire	*wonder (at)*, III. IV. 135.
affect	*like*, II. V. 21
affection'd	*affected (or ambitious)*, II. III. 132.
affections	*emotions*, I. I. 37.
allow	*prove*, I. II. 61; allow'd = *licensed, permitted*, I. V. 80.
already	*fully prepared*, III. I. 85.
alter	*exchange*, II. V. 134.
anatomy	*dead body for dissection*, III. II. 53.
anticke	*quaint*, II. IV. 3.
approbation	*confirmation*, III. IV. 158.
aqua vite	*eau de vie, strong spirits*, II. V. 167.
argument	*matter, theme*, II. V. 128; *proof*, III. II. 9; *subject of dispute*, III. III. 34.
attend	*heed*, I. IV. 27; *await*, III. IV. 54.
ayword	*byeword, reproach*, II. III. 121 (usually emended to "nay-word", but either form is possible).
backe-tricke	*a backwards dance step*, I. III. 107.
bar	*tribunal, judgment*, III. IV. 125.
barrefull	*beset with obstacles*, I. IV. 43.
bawbling	*trifling*, V. I. 47.
bawcock	*beau coq, fine fellow*, III. IV. 101.
beguile	*while away*, III. III. 44; *deceive*, V. I. 137.
become	*accord with, befit*, I. II. 56.
bent	*intensity, tension (as of a drawn bow)*, II. IV. 40.
beshrew	*curse (used playfully)*, II. III. 73.
betimes	*early*, II. III. 2.
biddy	*childish name for a chicken*, III. IV. 103.
bird-bolt	*blunt arrow for shooting birds*, I. V. 79.
blazon	*description, as of a heraldic shield*, I. V. 264.
blow	*puff up, inflate*, II. V. 38.
bones	*bobbins*, II. IV. 48.
botcher	*rough tailor who does repairs*, I. V. 40.
branch'd	*decorated with figured patterns of leaves, etc.*, II. V. 42.

breach	*breakers, surf,* II. I. 18.
breast	*singing voice,* II. III. 17.
brock	*badger (presumably = stinker),* II. V. 90.
Brownist	*extreme Puritan, from Robert Brown, 16-cent. founder of Independency,* III. II. 26.
bum-Baylie	*sheriff's officer,* III. IV. 155.
Buttry barre	*serving hatch of wine-cellar,* I. III. 61.
Canarie	*sweet wine from Canary Islands,* I. III. 74.
canton	*canto, song,* I. V. 239.
caper	*a dance step, punning on the sauce served with mutton, which = whore,* I. III. 105.
Capilet	*name for a horse, from dialect "capul" = horse,* III. IV. 253.
carranto	*coranto, a dance of "sliding passages",* I. III. 112.
case	*skin, especially of animals,* V. I. 166.
Catayan	*Chinese, = cheat ("This mention of my lady is all a swindle"),* II. III. 69.
challenge (the field)	*challenge to a duel,* II. III. 114.
champian	*champaign, open country,* II. V. 135.
chantry	*private chapel,* IV. III. 24.
charracter	*face or features betokening moral qualities,* I. II. 53; *handwriting,* V. I. 346.
check	*to turn aside from the proper quarry in hawking,* II. V. 100.
cherrie-pit	*children's game with cherry stones,* III. IV. 104.
chev'rill	*kid-skin,* III. I. 11.
chuck	*chicken, term of endearment,* III. IV. 101.
cipresse, cypresse	*veil of black lawn,* III. I. 117; *a shroud of the same, or possibly a coffin of c. wood,* II. IV. 56.
civill	*sedate,* III. IV. 4.
clodde-pole	*numskull,* III. IV. 166.
cloyment	*satiety,* II. IV. 100.
cockatrice	*basilisk, serpent with cock's head which kills at a glance,* III. IV. 171.
cockney	*(cock's egg), milksop,* IV. I. 12.
codling	*small unripe apple,* I. V. 139.
coffer	*money,* III. IV. 308.
colours, feare no	*fear nothing, probably of a foeman's flag; also = excuses,* I. V. 5.
come neere	*begin to understand,* III. IV. 60.
comedian	*stage-player,* I. V. 160.
comfortable	*comforting,* I. V. 194.
commodity	*parcel, consignment,* III. I. 39.
competent	*admissible, adequate,* III. IV. 219.
competitor	*confederate,* IV. II. 9.
complection	*natural constitution and/or appearance,* II. IV. 28.
comptible	*(answerable, hence) sensitive, susceptible,* I. V. 154.
con	*memorize,* I. V. 153.

conceited	*having formed a notion or opinion*, III. IV. 259.
confine	*restrict, with special reference to dress*, I. III. 8.
consanguinious	*kinsman*, II. III. 70.
consonancy	*consistency*, II. V. 112.
constant (question)	*consistent discussion, rationally conducted*, IV. II. 44.
conster	*construe, explain*, III. I. 51.
convents	*is convenient*, V. I. 381.
countie	*count* (title), I. V. 273.
coxcombe	*head*, V. I. 178; *fool*, V. I. 205.
coystrill	(*groom*), *knave*, I. III. 35.
cozier	*cobbler*, II. III. 81.
credite	*opinion, belief*, IV. III. 6.
crowner	*coroner*, I. V. 117.
curst	*petulant, perverse*, III. II. 34.
curtesie	*formality*, I. V. 181.
curtsies	*makes courtesy, bows*, II. V. 55.
cut	*term of abuse = common horse (gelding, or cut-tail)*, II. III. 166.
dally nicely	*play subtly (also, toy amorously)*, III. I. 13.
damaske	*blush-red colour*, II. IV. 115.
deceiveable	*deceptive, misleading*, IV. III. 21.
deere	*grievous, dire*, V. I. 64.
deliver	*make known, disclose*, I. II. 43; *utter message of*, V. I. 292.
denay	*denial*, II. IV. 128.
deplore	*tell with grief*, III. I. 159.
determinate	*intended*, II. I. 9.
dexteriously	*dexterously*, I. V. 52.
dimension	*bodily proportion*, I. V. 229; *body*, V. I. 238.
dishonest	*unchaste, lewd*, I. V. 36, IV. II. 29; *lacking honour*, III. IV. 351.
dismount	*remove, draw (of sword)*, III. IV. 199.
distemper	*infect, taint*, II. I. 4, I. V. 78.
divulg'd	*spoken of, reported*, I. V. 228.
dogge	*adept*, II. III. 56–8 (*punning on dog = animal, and = device for gripping*).
ducat(e)	*a gold or silver coin of varying value, in the 16th cent. worth about 6s 8d*, I. III. 20.
element	*sky, open air*, I. I. 27; *one of the four elements*, I. V. 244, II. III. 8; *sphere of life*, III. IV, 110; *sphere of thought*, III. I. 53.
estate	*rank, position*, I. II. 45, I. III. 95.
estimable wonder	*admiration in judging*, II. I. 23.
event	*result*, II. III. 155.
expresse	*reveal*, II. I. 12; *expressure = expression*, II. III. 140.
extent	(*seizure of property*), *assault*, IV. I. 48.
extracting	(*a play on "distracting"*), *drawing one out of one's wits*, V.I. 283.
extravagancie	*vagrancy, wandering*, II. I. 10.

fadge	*fit, turn out*, II. II. 30.
fat	*dull, gross*, V. I. 104.
fault	*loss of scent in hunting*, II. V. III.
favour	*appearance, look (punning on* "by your leave"*)*, II. IV. 24–6.
fertill	*abundant*, I. V. 223.
flesh'd	*experienced in sword-play (from the thrusting of a weapon into flesh)*, IV. I. 35.
fond	*dote*, II. II. 31.
forgive	*excuse*, I. V. 169.
forme (of my intent)	*outward purpose*, I. II. 57; *impression as of seal*, II. II. 27; *formal = sane, mentally normal*, II. V. 103.
fraught	*freight, cargo*, V. I. 54.
free	*innocent, easy in mind (of lace-makers)*, II. IV. 48.
from	*outside the sphere of*, I. V. 167; *not in accordance with*, V. I. 332.
fustian	*(coarse cloth), worthless, rubbishy*, II. V. 95.
galliard	*quick lively dance*, I. III. 112.
gard, out of his	*without means of defence*, I. V. 74.
gaskins	*galligaskins, breeches or hose*, I. V. 22.
gecke	*dupe*, V. I. 343.
generous	*high-minded*, I. V. 78.
genius	*(familiar spirit), spiritual nature*, III. IV. 115.
giddily	*carelessly*, II. IV. 84.
good life	*(?) jollification (taken by Andrew to mean* "moral sobriety"*)*, II. III. 34.
graine, in	*fast-dyed*, I. V. 206.
greene and yellow	*pale and sallow*, II. IV. 116.
greeke	*buffoon*, IV. I. 15.
grize	*step*, III. I. 121.
gust	*zest, relish*, I. III. 27.
habit	*dress, garb*, II. V. 143.
haggard	*untrained hawk, caught when adult*, III. I. 59.
heate	*(?) natural body temperature*, I. V. 115.
hob, nob	*(hab, nab), have it, have it not, come what may*, III. IV. 213.
houskeeper	*house-holder*, IV. II. 8.
hull	*lie or drift without using sails*, I. V. 177.
humour	*caprice*, I. IV. 4.
hyperbolicall	*turbulent, vehement*, IV. II. 23.
importance	*importunity*, V. I. 364.
incredulous	*unbelievable*, III. IV. 73.
inevitable	*physically unavoidable*, III. IV. 243.
inlarge	*release*, V. I. 280.
invention	*literary inventiveness*, III. II. 35; *composition*, V. I. 333; *ingenuity*, V. I. 344.

jade	*mock*, II. V. 139.
jealious	*anxious*, IV. III. 27.
jealousie	*suspicion, anxiety*, III. III. 8.
jet	*strut*, II. V. 27.
jumpe	*agree*, V. I. 253.
kicke-chawses	*quelques choses, trifles*, I. III. 100.
labell'd	*attached as codicil to a will*, I. V. 214.
lapsed	*(?) taken by surprise*, III. III. 38.
leasing	*lying*, I. V. 83.
legge	*(probably) graceful bow, obeisance*, II. III. 18.
lemon	*leman, mistress, sweetheart*, II. III. 22.
lenton	*lenten, sour, meagre*, I. V. 8.
lets	*hinders*, V. I. 250.
list	*limit, extreme bound*, III. I. 71.
little, drawne in	*contracted into small compass*, III. IV. 77.
lymde	*snared*, III. IV. 68.
manakin	*little man (contemptuously)*, III. II. 44.
maugre	*despite*, III. I. 148.
mettle (metal) of India	*gold*, II. V. 11.
misprision	*mistake, perhaps with erroneous sense of "wrongful arrest"*, I. V. 48.
modest	*moderate*, I. V. 157.
motion	*emotion, desire*, II. IV. 17; *proposal*, III. IV. 254.
motley	*fool's traditional dress, a long coat usually of greenish mixture*, I. V. 49.
mouse	*term of childish endearment*, I. V. 54.
mute	*silent onlooker, probably in theatrical sense*, I. II. 64.
naturall	*idiot*, I. III. 25, cp. II. III. 75.
non-regardance	*disregard, contempt*, V. I. 117.
numbers	*metre*, II. V. 88.
Nuntio	*official messenger*, I. IV. 28.
old age	*antique times*, II. IV. 51.
other gates	*otherwise*, V. I. 192.
owe	*own, possess*, I. V. 282; *be indebted*, II. IV. 104.
part	*lot, allotted portion*, II. IV. 60; (pl.) *possessions*, II. IV. 83.
pass upon	*make a fool of*, III. I. 37, V. I. 352.
passage	*act, incident*, III. II. 61.
peevish(ly)	*foolish(ly)*, I. V. 272, II. II. 11.
perchance	*perhaps*, I. II. 5; *by chance, luckily*, I. II. 6.
perdie	*indeed (= by God)*, IV. II. 70.
perpend	*attend, consider*, V. I. 299.

personage   *appearance, especially stature,* I . V. 137.
pia-mater   (*membrane around the*) *brain,* I. V. 99.
pitch   *height, excellence,* I. I. 12.
poast   *messenger, courier,* I. V. 255.
point devise   *perfectly correct,* II. V. 138.
points   *laces for fastening hose,* I. V. 20.
politician   *cunning schemer,* II. III. 69.
position   *arrangement,* II. V. 104.
possesse   *inform,* II. III. 124.
possest   *mad,* III. IV. 8.
practise, /ice (sb.)   *method,* I. II. 13; *plot,* V. I. 352.
prank   *adorn,* II. IV. 86.
pregnant   *resourceful, ready,* II. II. 25, III. I. 83.
present   *money on hand,* III. IV. 307; this present = *a moment ago,* I. V. 204; presently = *immediately,* III. IV. 173.
presuppos'd   *suggested beforehand,* V. I. 350.
prevented   *forestalled,* III. I. 78.
private   *privacy,* III. IV. 81.
profound heart   (?) *clever lady,* or perhaps *from the bottom of my heart,* I. V. 161.
proofe   *experience,* III. I. 121.
proper   *handsome,* II. II. 26; *own,* V. I. 316.
propertied   *treated as an insensible object,* (?) *stowed away like a theatrical property,* IV. II. 85.
propriety   *personal identity,* V. I. 147.

quicke   *lively, vigorous,* I. I. 9.
quit   *release from service,* V. I. 318.

receiving   *receptiveness, understanding,* III. I. 116.
recollected   *remembered, studied,* II. IV. 5.
recommend   *commit, entrust,* V. I. 85.
record   *recollection,* V. I. 247.
recover   *restore, save,* II. I. 32; *gain, obtain,* II. III. 163.
regard   *look, glance,* II. V. 60; demure travaile of r. = *gravely scanning the company one by one,* II. V. 48.
reliques   *antiquities,* III. III. 20.
rellish   *meaning, suggestion,* IV. I. 55.
renegatho   *turncoat, especially one who adopts Islam,* III. II. 60.
retention   *stability, constancy,* II. IV. 97; *holding back,* V. I. 75.
revolve   *consider,* II. V. 122.
romane (hand)   *italic style of handwriting, newly fashionable,* III. IV. 27.
round   *plain-spoken,* II. III. 85.
rudesbey   *ruffian, oaf,* IV. I. 46.

sacke   *sherry* (burnt s. is sherry and sugar heated), II. III. 168.
sad   *serious,* III. IV. 4.

scathfull	*harmful*, V. I. 49.
scruple	*(apothecary's weight,* hence) *minute portion;* also *doubt, objection,* III. IV. 72.
season	*preserve, as with brine,* I. I. 31.
semblative	*resembling,* Shn. coinage, I. IV. 35.
severall	*separate,* II. II. I S.D.
sheepe-biter	*sneaking rogue, especially woman-hunter,* II. V. 5.
shent	*scolded,* IV. II. 96.
sheriffes post	*post set up as sign of authority at the door of a mayor or sheriff,* I. V. 130.
shrewdly	*cruelly,* V. I. 352.
shrewishly	*sharply,* I. V. 141.
silly (sooth)	*innocent (truth),* II. IV. 49.
simulation	*veiled meaning, device,* II. V. 119.
sinister	*malicious, unjust,* I. V. 154.
sinke-a-pace	*(cinque pace), galliard of five steps,* I. III. 113.
skillesse	*inexperienced,* III. III. 9.
skipping	*skittish,* I. V. 175.
snecke up	*be hanged to you,* II. III. 84.
speake	*(?) play instrumental music,* I. II. 60. *Cp.* "discourse", *Hamlet,* III. II. 374.
sonnet	*any short poem or song (in this case, a ballad),* III. IV. 21.
spinster	*spinner,* II. IV. 47.
spleene	*(seat of laughter), merriment,* III. II. 58.
squash	*unripe pea-pod,* I. V. 139.
state	*rank, status,* I. V. 248; *ceremonious speech or behaviour,* II. III. 132; *chair of state,* II. V. 40.
still	*always,* II. IV. 31.
stocke	*stocking,* I. III. 118.
stone-bow	*cross-bow for shooting stones,* II. V. 41.
stoope	*stoup, drinking vessel of two quarts,* II. III. 12.
stout	*proud, haughty,* II. V. 144.
strange	*distant, reserved,* II. V. 144; *strangeness = reserve,* IV. I. 13.
stucke (sb.)	*thrust,* III. IV. 243.
substractors	*calumniators* (perversion of "detractors"), I. III. 29.
suited	*clothed,* V. I. 234.
supportance	*assistance, sake,* III. IV. 264; *supporter = prop,* I. V. 130.
surprize	*assail,* I. IV. 25.
swabber	*sailor (who washes deck),* I. V. 177.
swarth	*(swathe), heap,* II. III. 133.
swayes levell	*rules properly,* also *keeps equipoise, as a balance,* I I. IV. 33.
sweet and twentie	*term of endearment, apparently meaning* "sweet, and twenty times sweet", [I. III. 47.
tabor	*drum,* III. I. 2.
tall	*goodly, valiant,* I. III. 17.
tang	*utter in a ringing tone,* II. V. 128.

Tartar	*Tartarus, Hell,* II. V. 175.
taxation	*imposition, demand,* I. V. 183.
tender (vb.)	*have regard for,* V. I. 122; *proffer,* V. I. 111.
testrill	*tester, from "teston", sixpence,* II. III. 30.
tilly vally	*pish tush!, an exclamation of contempt (favoured by the wife of Sir Thomas More),* II. III. 71.
tray-trip	*dice game, depending on the three (trey),* II. V. 161.
tricke	*custom, habit,* II. V. 129.
triplex	*triple musical time,* V. I. 33.
tucke	*rapier,* III. IV. 199.
undertaker	*one who takes up a challenge,* III. IV. 281.
unhatch'd	*(? = unhacked), unused,* III. IV. 209.
unprizable	*valueless, not worth taking as a prize,* V. I. 48.
unsound	*lacking in self-control,* III. IV. 312.
uppeshot	*final shot, conclusion,* IV. II. 65.
usurpe	*occupy wrongfully, counterfeit,* I. V. 164; *misuse,* I. V. 165.
venerable	*worthy of respect,* III. IV, 327.
vertues	*accomplishments,* I. III. 114.
Viol-de-gamboys	*bass viol, played between the legs,* I. III. 22.
vox	*declamation,* V. I. 296.
voyces	*repute,* I. V. 228.
wanton	*(of girls) unchaste, (of words) ambiguous, perhaps also with pun on "want(lack)-one",* III. I. 14, 18.
waters, for all	*ready for anything (precise sense obscure),* IV. I I. 58.
welkin	*sky,* II. III. 53, III. I. 53 (cp. "element").
whirlegigge	*revolving device, perhaps a top, and/or its motion,* V. I. 376.
winke	*close one's eyes,* V. I. 84.
wit	*inventiveness,* I. II. 63; *verbal dexterity,* I. V. 28; *clever man,* I. V. 29; *intelligence,* V. I. 210.
worth	*wealth,* III. III. 18.
yare	*swift, alert,* III. IV. 199.
zany	*assistant to a professional fool,* I. V. 76.